THE HUMILITY IMPERATIVE

THE
HUMILITY
IMPERATIVE

Effective Leadership in an Era of Arrogance

ESSAYS BY

DAVE BALTER

HOUNDSTOOTH
PRESS

THE HUMILITY IMPERATIVE
Effective Leadership in an Era of Arrogance

ISBN   978-1-5445-0811-5 *Hardcover*
            978-1-5445-0810-8 *Paperback*
            978-1-5445-0809-2 *Ebook*

Please note that I'd have much preferred to have forgone the 's' in Brussels sprouts. Brussel sprouts is cleaner—yet regrettably, incorrect. The English language is indeed a most quirky beast.

At least we'll know where these delicious sprouts originated. Brussels. With an 's.'

Speaking of s's, this book is for Sarah, for whom I'm forever grateful.

CONTENTS

To read with great pleasure and get the most out of each chapter, visit thehumilityimperative.com.

THE JOURNEY (SO FAR)

Many chapters in this book originated as articles in *Inc.*, *Forbes*, *Business Insider*, *Startup Grind*, *Hacker Noon*, and other publications. Authored between 2011 and 2019, they comprise elements of the startup journey at various intervals in the cycle. Over time, some themes have crystalized. In others, the words seemed to seek thinning or required clarification. In those cases, the text has been updated and refreshed.

For context-setting, be sure to orient to the original dates of publication in the header of each chapter and refer to this chart (a snapshot of my executive history).

COMPANY	ROLE	DURATION
Retrofit/360Merch	CEO	1996–2001
BzzAgent	CEO	2001–2010
dunnhumby (acquired BzzAgent)	Head of M&A and Venture Capital	2010–2014
dunnhumby Ventures	Managing Director	2013–2016
Smarterer	Exec Chair > CEO	2010–2014
Boston Seed Capital	Venture Partner > Venture Partner Emeritus	2011–Present
Intelligent.ly	Managing Director	2012–2018
Pluralsight (acquired Smarterer)	Head of Transactions	2014–2016
Mylestone	CEO	2016–2017
Flipside Crypto	CEO	2018–Present

INTRODUCTION

In 1066, William the Conqueror became the king of England.

He kicked off his reign by confiscating land from Saxon lords and allocating it to members of his own family—he also tossed a few acres to the Norman lords who helped him overthrow the country.

This was pretty much a major bummer for those who already lived on the land.

They were deemed common people. Peasants.

The designation bore more pain than unfortunate classification: they were required to provide services to the king, and for that, they received protection and were able to continue living in their feeble huts.

Of course, King Willy wasn't all bad. He threw lord-like bashes for those in the upper class. And, after choosing the best cuts of meat for his festivities, he passed on the scraps to the peasants. (Hey, c'mon, it would be hard for them to provide services if they starved, right?)

These leftover meats, they had a name. They were called umbles.

And that's where the word humble originated. Over the course of time, humble became associated with anything deferential. Indeed, humble pie is now what you eat when you exist in a lowly station.

Humility, thus, is what you have when you are humble—providing some logic to why humility is defined as having a modest view of your own importance.

Fast-forward a few centuries and here I sit contemplating the very nature of humility. Frankly, it confuses me.

I've run seven startup companies. One was acquired for $60 million and another for $150 million.

One of my companies was the cover story of a *New York Times Magazine* article.

For years, I served on the global executive team of a $1 billion revenue company with 2,500 employees.

I'm a (slightly reformed) venture capitalist and have personally invested in north of fifty startup companies on my own.

Early in my career I was unequipped to balance my abilities with the perception of myself. I can imagine a few folks considered me a narcissist. Arrogant. An egomaniac.

A complete and utter asshole.

But over time, the sharp edges have dulled. I've received executive coaching and I've been part of team exercises that border on therapy sessions. With a bit of success, I no longer have to race to prove results; I've become more comfortable in the marathon versus the sprint.

But in order to build a company, one has to inspire a team. In order to woo investors and manage boards of directors, one has to make strong decisions. In order to invest capital in someone else's startup, one has to have conviction. In all cases, one has to have confidence.

Which begs the question: can one be confident and have humility at the same time?

The Humility Imperative—the concept—is the assignment of that question.

In order to explore that, one needs to understand that humility may be intended in one's heart, but only becomes genuine if it is reflected through the thoughts of others. The lessons are a reminder that every interaction—both professional and personal—is the lens by which your own intents become clear.

Humility is an imperative. It lives in the eye of the beholder.

The Humility Imperative—the book—delivers authentic, raw evidence that building anything requires constant attentiveness to interpersonal dynamics.

Central to that are the professional relationships that fuel any business growth: teams, investors, managers, peers, and clients, as well as current, potential, and even ex-employees. Many chapters of the book focus there.

Yet those relationships pale compared to the significance of the personal relationships required for the leadership journey—the individuals who provide unseen support, criticism, and love. "The significant other." "The spouse." Nay, the passenger who is along for the ride, whether they like it or not. While often overlooked in the broader narrative of stories of success and failure, the impact of these relationships can't be simplified, obfuscated, or overstated.

Building any company is like guiding a rowboat in the middle of the ocean: massive swells and troughs require one to hold on tightly while bounding between sheer terror and supreme elation. You may find the chapters of this book follow that rhythm. Be prepared to climb aboard.

The rises and falls may be unintended consequences of the journey, but the silver lining is that they force behaviors to ensure execution through strength of leadership.

Those behaviors often require confidence. And *always* require humility.

BRUSSELS SPROUTS (A LOVE STORY)

ORIGINALLY PUBLISHED NOVEMBER 20, 2019

I opened the bathroom door gently, whispering 'Hodgie?'

Somewhere within, a guttural groan.

The clock said 1:32 a.m.

Brussels sprouts for dinner. And she had clearly been ill.

Through the hazy darkness—the light of the moon barely sneaking through the blinds of the bathroom window—I could see the silhouette of her splayed form on the ground. She was on her back, hair wild, a blonde octopus.

'Hodgie?'

She moaned, and seemed alive. I closed the door and went back to bed.

* * *

Early bedtime, 9:45 p.m.

In the kitchen, there was a faint tangy whiff of Brussels sprouts still hanging in the air post dinner. Whatever it was, it was more than just a scent. It was an aura, filling the room with an electric, uncomfortable energy.

My mind wouldn't settle; the clock beamed 1 a.m. A mental calculation and reluctant acceptance of only five hours of sleep before the alarm rang.

Hodgie shot straight up in bed.

"Sweating," she said, notifying no one in particular. She stumbled, half-crawled out of bed and into the darkness of the hallway.

* * *

Brussels sprouts and I have something of a history.

Roll back the clock a decade ago, and you'd find me home alone with our first child; I had just tucked the three-year-old into bed and was settling in for the night.

I rooted through the refrigerator for something to cook for dinner. Brussels sprouts, yes!

My wife had a knack for making the best grilled Brussels: a heavy dose of oil, salt, pepper, and some other spices—then a good, crisp roasting in the oven.

Yeah, I can do that, I thought.

I might have smoked a joint.

I took the bag from the fridge and noticed it had about an inch of milky liquid in the bottom, likely the result of a good washing.

No matter. I emptied the bag, halved the sprouts, and popped them in the oven.

I ate a sailor's portion.

At about 2 a.m. I woke from a dream where I was vomiting. Then, I vomited. For about six hours.

Later, my wife noted that said Brussels sprouts had been in the fridge for about two months. That wasn't water from washing— it was the putrefaction of the vegetable soaking in its own rot.

* * *

Hodgie eventually returned to bed. It was nearing 2:30 a.m. and I'd been checking on her every fifteen minutes (lightly tapping on the door, avoiding opening it at all costs). She was wearing a heavy hoodie and had buried herself under all of the covers.

A short twenty minutes later she was up, offering that she was freezing and needed to take a shower. I listened to the water running for a while, and it crossed my mind that she could possibly pass out. Would there be a crash? Would it be a silent fall? Would the water just flow on and on and on, inconsiderately scalding her?

Eventually the water stopped and she came back to bed.

I still couldn't sleep. Then, 4 a.m. rounded the corner.

It sounded like Hodgie was downstairs. I lay still, trying to figure out what was happening. Now it sounded like she was upstairs again, back in the bathroom maybe.

Then: a bone-chilling sound. Two gloopy, heavy, muffled thumps.

Thwock. Thwock.

They were about three seconds apart and sounded like sacks of potatoes falling off the back of a truck. Then, dead still silence.

'Hodgie?' I called out.

Nothing.

I pulled my covers back and hustled into the bathroom. The door was open; it was dark.

'Hodgie?'

I turned on the lights. She was swathed in a layer of sweat-shirts and sweatpants and slumped—no, cratered—between the toilet and the vanity.

She wasn't moving. As a matter of fact, she was completely unconscious.

* * *

I yelled. Then I slapped her face a few times because they do that in the movies. Then I tried to prop open her eyes. Blank, glassy.

She released a snore, which was sharply cut short by her constricted windpipe. At least it was proof that she was breathing.

"HODGIE?"

911, fast, like a blur. I'm pumped full of adrenaline, hardly thinking, just reacting.

The seconds pass—ninety seconds in and she's still completely unresponsive. I try to move her to the floor, but she's completely jammed, legs and arms awkwardly trapped. I was yelling at 911 to hurry.

"Sir," they repeat, "we need your address."

* * *

Just as I was hanging up the phone, Hodgie's eyes fluttered open. She was now face down on the bathroom floor, blinking spastically, like a deer clipped by a speeding car. It took twelve frighteningly long minutes for the ambulance to arrive. I'd reluctantly sprinted downstairs to the windows near the street to keep an eye out for it. Every minute, I yelled up to her to say something. I told her to not fall asleep.

The street was awash in flashing blue and red lights. The EMTs slowly climbed the stairs; just another home, another person in distress. "Nice house," one of them muttered. They left the front door wide open. Irrelevant to the matter at hand.

They smelled of cigarettes and had accents straight out of *The Departed*. They were young, but unflappable. One of them tended to Hodgie, taking her blood pressure and passing her a tiny portable bag in case she became ill. The other took me aside and pulled a tiny notebook from his breast pocket, a move no doubt executed thousands of times before.

"What's her name? What happened?"

"Is it possible she's pregnant?" (No.)

I told him she'd been on antibiotics for a cold for four days— Amoxicillin. That tonight, we had Brussels sprouts and she took some NyQuil. He scribbled.

"Red chair," the other eventually called out, the code language of an action. The other trudged back down the stairs.

They slowly raised her to her feet; she was white as a ghost. They settled her into the newly arrived portable red chair and covered her in blankets.

She said she felt like she was underwater.

She told me she was going to need shoes. "Which ones?" I asked stupidly.

They carried her down two flights of stairs and I followed them to the waiting ride. They moved her to a Stryker portable gurney and raised her into the ambulance. I hopped in, embarrassed that for some reason I found it kinda cool. The doors slammed shut and so began them arguing with Hodgie about which hospital they'd go to.

"MGH," she said.

"No, ma'am, Boston Medical."

"I don't want to go there."

"We have to go to the closest hospital." They were firm, but
cautious.

"MGH."

A pause. "We can take you to Tufts, but not MGH."

If she had her act together—even halfway—Hodgie would
have fought them into submission. But she couldn't muster
the strength. Tufts it was.

* * *

At the hospital, the EMTs downloaded to the staff.

"Is she pregnant?" the intake woman asked.

Behind her, a group of security guards were fist-bumping and
chuckling at some inside joke. Another cadre of staffers were
having what looked like lunch. Someone on a gurney nearby
was asked if he heard the same voices he did when he was
admitted last summer.

"No, she's not. She's not pregnant," the EMT said.

The EMTs scooted. Now, we were in a private room. A nurse
and then a doctor came in ten minutes apart. Each asked the

exact same set of questions as if trying to trip us up. They hooked Hodgie up to a bag of fluids. When that drip finished, they'd begin another one.

"Do you think it's a reaction to the antibiotics, mixed with NyQuil?"

"Or a stomach bug. The dreaded norovirus?"

No medical expert committed to anything specific.

Someone in the next room was screaming and vomiting endlessly, loudly.

They explained that she passed out because she stimulated the vagus nerve from intense stomach pain. Apparently, it triggered her heart rate and blood pressure to drop suddenly and caused her body to "auto-rest."

Two hours later, dawn broke. Hodgie said her stomach still hurt but she'd be OK to go home. Next, a flurry of paperwork and payments.

They weren't in any rush, but we both privately worried that we wouldn't make it back in time to take the trash out.

* * *

Hodgie sometimes does Hodgie things.

Once she made breakfast, and left the flame on the stove on high as she hustled out to work. When we got home eight hours later, the pan was bright white, so hot that the color had just melted away.

Once she ordered some beanbag chairs for our roof, but couldn't be bothered to measure the space or think on the sizing of the chairs. Turned out the beanbags were massive—nearly five times the required size—and she had ordered four of them. We avoided calls from the delivery service for days.

"Eventually they'll just return to sender," she said, uninterested.

Another time, Hodgie left the house while I was in the shower. On the way out, forgetting that I was still there, she punched in the code for the security system. When I reached for a towel, the motion detectors kicked in and I was attacked by the ear-piercing shrill of the alarm. I only barely averted killing myself running up and down the stairs thinking the house was on fire.

These things are Hodgie things.

* * *

The EMTs I can't shake. I imagine what it's like to be them, climbing the stairs to some un-foregone conclusion. I'm Nicolas Cage in 1999's *Bringing Out the Dead*. The deranged EMT trying to maintain his sanity over three delirious nights.

The night is behind us, and yet it lingers. Flashbacks are like snapshots of movie frames. Moments rise like the swell of a river pounded on by a terrifying storm, lapping at the banks, eager to burst over the sides.

I am wildly in love with Hodgie, but the patterns of daily life often numb the acuteness of that.

And yet with this particular event, I am deeply affected and newly present.

I note to Hodgie that she almost delivered the ultimate Hodgie.

"What would that be?" she asks.

"It would be hitting your head on the vanity after passing out, then dying soundlessly on the bathroom floor. One final Hodgie to beat out all other Hodgies. It would be the Hodgie mic drop."

I wondered...then who would I eat Brussels sprouts with?

THE HUMILITY IMPERATIVE

ORIGINALLY PUBLISHED IN *INC.*, JUNE 23, 2011

This is a message to every entrepreneur, CEO, and leader: dig a hole, throw your ego into it, and pour concrete on top. Find humility instead.

Hello, my name is Dave Balter, and I'm a CEO who used to be utterly ego-driven.

(There. I said it.)

This ego gave me the confidence to be a great leader but also nearly destroyed BzzAgent, the pioneering word-of-mouth company I founded. Had I not dramatically adjusted my leadership style, in all likelihood my partners and I wouldn't have found our way to a successful exit. (In the spring of 2011, Tesco subsidiary dunnhumby acquired BzzAgent.)

I believe—due to an inflated market, easy cash, and entrepreneur glorification—that there are thousands of companies destined to fail if their leaders, who may feel like business deities today, don't immediately turn their hubris into humility.

BzzAgent Harvard Business School case, 2006

I learned the hard way that a CEO isn't God. I launched BzzAgent, my fourth startup, in 2001. By 2005, I had a tiger by the tail: venture capitalists were wooing us, competitors studied us, and the media swooned. BzzAgent was featured as the cover story of *New York Times Magazine*, and the company was the subject of two Harvard Business School cases. I was labeled a genius, and I believed it. In 2004 we generated $3 million in revenue. That rocketed to $8 million—profitably—in 2005. Our clients included some of the biggest companies in the world, from Procter & Gamble and L'Oréal to Penguin Publishing. In January 2006, the company closed a groundbreaking $14 million round of institutional financing at a $54 million valuation.

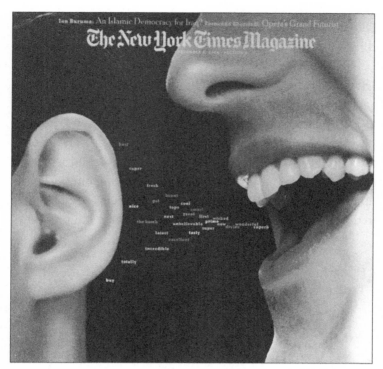

BzzAgent NY Times Magazine cover story, December 2004

Concurrently, my entire style evolved from confident to cocky. When I heard rumblings that members of my family were put off by my "inflated self-worth because of BzzAgent," I chalked it up to being shortsighted. When I interviewed job candidates, I was less conversational and more confrontational. I refused to attend conferences that didn't choose me as a keynote speaker. By the time 2007 rolled around, I was blinded by my own press and felt BzzAgent was unstoppable. Sure, I thought I listened to others, but looking back I realize now that the only voices I heard were the ones in my head. I made every product decision, shunned investment overtures, and ignored competitors as wannabes and copycats. I believed my vision was untouchable.

These were signals of CEO behavior that could doom any company, even in good times.

Then came 2009. The recession started to pull against BzzAgent. It was a tough period for many businesses, but it was especially hard for us because of my outsized ego and the way I was leading the company. New rivals emerged and social media platforms evolved. My attitude prevented us from seeing changes coming until they were choking our business. Innovative clients who wanted to try new concepts didn't get it. In the world according to Balter, there was only Balter's view.

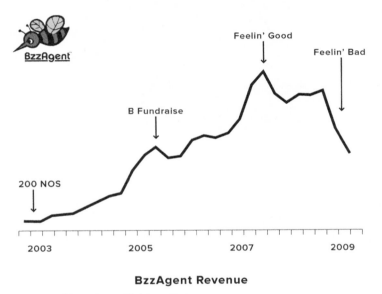

BzzAgent Revenue

The impact of the market—and hubris—on BzzAgent revenue

BzzAgent's revenues went into a tailspin, which made our budgeted expenses unsustainable. In 2009, we let go of more than fifty people—nearly half of our staff—in three separate rounds of reductions. Talented 'A' players who weren't let go ended up taking other jobs. My partners and I strategized and debated and fought and, in scarier moments, wondered if it was the end of the road for BzzAgent.

Board meetings became tense as we recognized the problems stretched beyond the economic climate but struggled to identify the root cause. After one such meeting in early 2010, our chairman pulled me aside and said it was the worst board meeting we'd had in five years—but not because of how the business was faring.

My attitude was the problem.

That was the wake-up moment.

THE HUMILITY IMPERATIVE: HOW I CHANGED

I was forced to grasp that I didn't have all the answers. In fact, I had to face the fact that I was pretty lousy at some things, like the process of product development, for instance. Humbled, I started to change my mindset. I became a student and a sponge. I sought and analyzed as many different perspectives, management styles, and corporate structures as possible. I joined a CEO group and learned to listen to and communicate with a dozen other leaders who had experienced similar challenges and understood the reality of needing to evolve.

I changed the way I made decisions, too. Rather than just saying I valued input from employees and peers, I followed their opinions. I turbocharged BzzAgent's social media efforts and embraced social networks as an important tool for our volunteer citizen marketeers. I even started housing startup companies in our Boston office. From individuals to recently funded companies, I literally surrounded the company with other innovators, ideas, and points of view. Gradually, my inward gaze turned outward.

With persistence, BzzAgent came out leaner, better, smarter, and stronger. While the effort we made to redefine our vision and become a client-driven business helped us tremendously, none of it would have happened had I not embraced vulnerability and humility.

I worry now that other entrepreneurs are about to repeat my mistakes. There has been a bubble swelling in the rich and frothy startup market for the past few years. A new class of CEOs and entrepreneurs are finding it easy to get funding from top-tier venture capitalists (VCs) or executives from Google or Chinese conglomerates. Their names pop up in *TechCrunch*, *Axios*, and *The Information*, and they're on the map. They're being recognized at CES (a yearly consumer technology business conference) or invited to private offsites in Vail or slapping one another on the back over bacon and eggs at Henrietta's Table, a Cambridge, Massachusetts, gathering spot where VCs and entrepreneurs mingle.

Cheerleaders will disappear, rivals will emerge, and the market will become less forgiving. Arrogant CEOs won't see the changes coming.

THE HUMILITY IMPERATIVE: HOW TO MAKE IT WORK FOR YOU

The humility imperative is simple: if you're an ego-fueled leader, find humility today, before it's too late. Disregard the fawning fanboys and king-like power you feel right now. Instead, choose to recognize that your place in the universe is no more important than anyone else's. Know you can learn from every single interaction—no matter the person's credentials. Understand that your competitors are smart—perhaps (gasp!) even smarter than you. Believe that media glory is fleeting. Remember that fundraising is a tactic, not a strategy. Your reputation isn't forever golden because VC firm a16z backed you.

Here's what matters more: you treat your employees with kindness; you are willing to be wrong; and—yes, this is hard—you share the spotlight.

Seth B. Minkin's "CEO Burying Ego," 2011

Having trouble admitting your ego is out of control? Ask your family, friends, or most-trusted adviser. Find someone willing to tell you straight. Your business will be much better for it, and you'll truly have the opportunity to create something great. Humility will prepare you for the endurance test to come. It will give you the flexibility to create a business that can thrive in good times and survive the bad.

Have humility, or your hubris will have you.

ARE YOU THE OCD EA?

ORIGINALLY PUBLISHED MARCH 25, 2013

Charm: Capable of enrapturing and inspiring coworkers, senior execs, international dignitaries, llamas, ocelots, infants, restaurant managers, and parking lot attendants.

Attitude: Positive, tenacious, curious, fun, inviting, and warm. No BS.

Qualities: MUST. LOVE. PRESSURE.

Time: You're ready for game time *anytime*. 9–5 = 4.

Skills: Email badass and calendaring aficionado. Typo slayer. Judo travel planner and airline seat juggler. Capable of finding Bangladeshi coffee in St. Louis, and familiar with how to tip in Moscow.

Disorders: Must love details so much you verge on OCD. Arachnophobia acceptable, but less advantageous.

Discretion: Can you keep a secret? Good, so can I.

Fun: Must know it, have it, and be able to inspire it.

Compensation: Money. Insane amounts of vacation. Tax-advantageous savings programs. Government-funded doctor's visits. Free rims for your new glasses.

Communication: Banter me at dave@flipsidecrypto.com.

[This role was filled by the incomparable Kate Brigham, who provided six years of two additional right hands, countless hours of witty repartee, and a therapist's lifetime of counseling.]

YOUR MANY, MANY GAPS—AND HOW YOU FILL THEM

ORIGINALLY PUBLISHED IN *STARTUP GRIND*, SEPTEMBER 20, 2017

Nearly a decade ago, a member of my executive team walked into my office with a no-win situation.

Here's what it looked like:

> *I either restructured his ownership in the company—essentially doubling what he had been granted already—or he packed up his bag of tricks, shook some hands, wished everyone well, and exited stage left.*

Providing him the equity he was asking for was impossible; he would end up with more ownership than any other executive. Not to mention it would require a board vote, an increase to the option pool, and dilution for every single person in the company.

He was valuable but, well...not to everyone else's detriment.

That said, the thought of him leaving the company was nothing short of a nightmare. He was an incredibly talented individual who was literally the central nervous system of the business. He oversaw our finances, employee operations, and internal client processes. He chaired our team meetings. He managed every vendor relationship. Losing him would most certainly be a step backward.

And—get this—we were smack-dab in the middle of selling the company—and he was the one responsible for the transaction.

This distinguished gentleman was also a particularly stiff and fearless negotiator. I guess the bull's-eye timing of this "offer" would probably make that obvious.

I called our chairman in a panic. With venom, I explained the situation. Without this exec, we would end up in a tailspin, and our M&A transaction would fall apart. We could very well go out of business.

Our chairman listened. He asked a few clarifying questions. He noted that this particular executive, no matter how we looked at it, on pretty much every dimension, would be a major loss and a possible crushing blow to the company. After that, he offered the following:

> "Let him walk," he said. "No matter how irreplaceable you believe anyone is, somehow, the gaps always fill in."

* * *

If you find a spare moment, watch *Under Great White Northern Lights*, the ninety-two-minute documentary about the White Stripes' 2007 summer tour of Canada. It's particularly special because the band intersperses major venue stops with random, obscure tiny gigs—on buses, in cafés, and for Indian tribal Elders who were both bewildered and appreciative of the band's garage-rock sound.

In the middle of the movie, Jack White offers his secret technique for bringing passion and massive energy to each show every night. With just two musicians—Jack mainly plays guitar and Meg mainly drums—there's an incredible amount of space to fill. The trick, Jack explains, is generating energy by forcing himself to work harder every night. Contrary to most musicians, who settle for well-rehearsed, comfortable efforts, he makes the music more difficult to achieve.

Case in point: with each show, he positions the piano an inch or two further away than the previous night.

That's right; he moves it *further away* from himself.

Then, in the frenzy of one of their songs, while Jack is playing guitar (completely destroying it, really) and belting out lyrics through the front-of-stage microphone, he realizes he needs to get to the piano to nail a chord for the melody, which is now positioned farther than it's ever been on the side of the stage. So he has to leap—literally hurdle—over to the piano, which is now more distant from him than ever before.

Every night, one inch. Then the next night, another inch. And another.

And it's that tension, Jack explains, that need to stretch, to dig deep—*to challenge his own ability*—that drives the music.

Just when he thinks he has no more room, he exceeds every element of his capability.

Jack White. Stretching. Pushing. Exceeding.

He filled in gaps he didn't even know he had.

* * *

In 2013, I had the fortune of sitting on the executive team of dunnhumby, a $1 billion revenue data analytics organization. My direct responsibilities included running a venture fund and M&A activities, but more broadly my responsibility was to work closely with this global team to run the business.

I joined this team after they acquired BzzAgent and had a few years of required employment to receive the earnout from that sale.

To say the role was overwhelming would be an understatement. Every eight weeks the executive team traveled to one of our global locations—Thailand, India, Poland, Paris, Oslo, London, and Cincinnati (oh yeah, what's up Cinci!)—and reviewed, debated, and strategized for a week.

Besides a travel regimen that put all of us in a constant fog of jet lag, preparation for this week often included a pre-read that could extend to north of 400 pages.

And, as if I needed more to do, at the time I was also serving as chairman of Smarterer, the machine-learning skill assessment business I'd founded in late 2010. While chairman duties required less time, they absolutely filled in any gaps in my schedule and mind space. Or, any gaps I thought I had.

Then, the unimaginable happened.

The CEO of Smarterer resigned; it wasn't sudden, but it did require immediate action to ensure the business didn't falter. We had less than a year of cash and no clear scalable revenue model, so Smarterer was unable to stand on its own.

We immediately tried to recruit a new CEO and talked to everyone we thought capable, but we were failing miserably. Every solid candidate seemed hesitant to join, for a myriad of reasons, the number one being "How can I be CEO if you're directly involved in the day-to-day of the business?"

I flew out to meet with the partner of our lead venture capital investor to discuss the situation. After a bit of light chatter, he turned to me and laid it right down:

"You sold us the vision, raised the money, and brought in the CEO. You got us into this mess. There are no more bullets left. Time to step up. You're the f*cking CEO now," he barked.

Three days later I approached the CEO of dunnhumby and let him know about the corner I'd backed myself into. There was no choice, I had to leave dunnhumby to take over Smarterer. He thought on the situation and then offered a suggestion that hadn't even crossed my mind: "Well, why don't you continue your duties here—and manage the Smarterer role too?"

It seemed ridiculous. Untenable on any level. A mental punishment.

But it was the only way to protect the investors in BzzAgent (my continued employment was a contingency for the earn-out) and the investors in Smarterer. If I was going to be a good corporate citizen, I really had no choice.

I promised myself I'd do it for only a year.

I restructured my schedule to remove any wasted time, shortened meetings by fifteen minutes each, used long flights to execute on project plans, and delegated tasks well beyond my typical micromanager scope.

Know what? Somehow it all worked. dunnhumby Ventures thrived and I was even given another project or three to manage. And, as if a perfectly delivered punchline, at the very end of that predetermined single year, Smarterer was acquired for a massive return for investors (more on this later).

Know how I made it all happen?

The gaps. I filled them in.

* * *

Fast-forward a few years and my hands were in a few projects. Other entrepreneurs and investors alike often asked the exact same question:

> *So, you run Mylestone as CEO and recently launched Flipside Crypto, a cryptocurrency analytics firm? These seem like two full-time jobs. How exactly do you do both?*

I'm not sure that's the right question.

If you're inspired, curious, and driven to deliver on any project—regardless of what is already on your plate—then there is always room.

- You might feel overwhelmed, but there are thousands of little gaps—little spaces that can be filled with some other effort—within your day that can be filled in.
- And, on top of that, there are probably dozens of items you could *remove* to create even more sizable gaps.
- And then there's the willingness—nay, the requirement—to always stretch to *find* the gaps you didn't even know you had.

The gaps, they always fill in. The gaps you didn't even know you had.

So really, the right question might be: What will you do to adapt, adjust, or refine in order to make room?

Which gaps will *you* fill in?

ALL VCS ARE DICKS

ORIGINALLY PUBLISHED IN *HACKER NOON*, OCTOBER 15, 2018

During one fundraising process, I spent forty-five minutes with a venture capitalist I'd never met before.

The meeting started with the usual feeling-each-other-out type of chatter: shared contacts, recent travels, weather.

With the effortlessness only possible of "meeting professionals," we transitioned to business.

First, an overview of their fund strategy (fintech), investment stage (seed/A), and capital structure (a few funds, $100 million). Then, seamlessly, to my current venture. We talked high-level thesis. I demonstrated our product.

There was a rhythm to our conversation. We had chemistry. We were warm and comfortable. Jamming.

Then he leaned forward, arms crossed on the table. He paused, peered out over his glasses, and dropped this gem:

   "Want to know the trouble with this industry?

"All venture capitalists are dicks.

"We have the money and strong opinions.

"But know what's even worse than that?

"All entrepreneurs. They suck."

His accent was thick, and it took me a moment to process the punchline.

In writing it seems obvious. But in person I was more reflective of the tear-down of the occupations than the clear association of the insults.

He had already moved on, but realizing maybe I hadn't connected the dots, he backtracked and took it for a second spin:

"Seriously, we're all dicks. But entrepreneurs..." Then, the pause...for emphasis. "They suck."

The rest of the meeting was as you'd expect. We continued our discussion on the business and their fund, and whether there was an opportunity to create value together.

But all of that was a blur. It was all irrelevant to the crushing weight of that brief interaction.

- In an era of #metoo, was a line crossed, and if so, which one? Exhibit one: a dick-sucking joke between two guys in a closed meeting. No women involved or mentioned. But, where five years ago this might have been shrugged off as harmless locker-room talk between bros, it's now heavy with meaning. Has my brain been rewired? Are my eyes now more fully opened?

- In a somewhat associated vein, the VC-to-entrepreneur power dynamic continues to be woefully imbalanced. We may have made some strides within gender boundaries (I'm pretty sure this particular VC would not have made that joke to a female entrepreneur), but not so much as it relates to the golden rule (you know: those with the gold...rule). More pointedly, if I'd made an attempt at that statement, the results would likely have been, well... career-limiting.

I left the meeting with a handshake and a smile and equal promises that we'd continue the dialogue.

I tried to forget it ever happened. It was, after all, just words in a private room.

But, weeks later, I still find myself recounting the story to others. It turns out it was one of the most remarkable moments in a trip full of remarkable moments.

I'm left wondering exactly how I should feel.

If anything at all.

KNOW THY ENEMY, BEFRIEND YOUR RIVALS

ORIGINALLY PUBLISHED IN *INC.*, JANUARY 30, 2012

Here's a truth: at BzzAgent, the word-of-mouth marketing firm I led as CEO from 2001 to 2010, I went to ridiculous extremes to obtain information about our competitors.

I scanned Crunchbase, studied websites, and downloaded mobile apps. I trolled shamelessly for gossip about our rivals' executive teams and star players. And occasionally, when I was really on my game, I'd hit pay dirt and obtain a competitor's proposal. When that happened, our team went to work. We dissected it for valuable bits of information about our opponents' pricing models, positioning, and capabilities. And it's this information that allowed us to accelerate our innovation, understand where our competitors were strong, and determine how we could exploit their weaknesses.

From one proposal, we learned that our flat-fee model was being devalued by another company's cost-per-engagement pricing. We created a strategy to counter that objection with clients and prospects. And a few years later, we got the inside scoop on a new opponent's practice of throwing in-home product-distribution parties for marketers and got ahead of the market by developing the next evolution of the concept.

We were also interested in information about our competitors' processes. For a while, one rival company responded to email inquiries by tersely exclaiming that they only accepted clients who had a minimum of $1 million to spend. Hey, we were happy to accept those that "just missed" that criterion. In another case, a company that tracks social influence positioned itself as a competitor to us, but inside information proved that their engineering-first culture could be perceived as unfriendly to clients. Our awareness of that issue was the foundation for a very lucrative partnership discussion.

As a strategy, this means more than the collection and dissection of as much information on your competitors as possible. Alongside minor cloak-and-dagger data gathering, you should also be developing real, personal relationships with people at all levels of your competitors' businesses. Just as much value—possibly even more—can come from a direct relationship. Why not identify and tackle common challenges and goals? Growing an industry is often about the sum of its parts. With a rival, you might create standards or align to compete against a regulation. Heck, you may even partner to win a big client.

And if you're leading an organization and aren't similarly fixated on both knowledge-gathering strategies, you're putting your company at great risk.

I wasn't always so obsessed. At one time, I thought BzzAgent was untouchable. I believed we could always stay one step ahead of the competition. I was convinced that what we did was often right and what our rivals did was often wrong. Of course we would continue to evolve and they would remain static.

But I was wrong.

Many a corporate pundit will tell you to just focus on your own business. Don't get distracted by the competition, they will say. In our case, we were so focused on ourselves that we failed to look up in time to see how things had evolved. We were the first entrant into the space in 2001, and for many years we were considered the only game in town. We didn't have to outpitch anyone. We just had to be us.

When competitors finally showed up around 2005, we mocked the fact that they weren't nearly as knowledgeable as we were. We were confident they lacked our experience. We thought their evolutions and variations of our model wouldn't significantly impact us. But by 2009, we found ourselves losing more projects than we were winning.

Competitors had learned how to pitch against us. Their innovations weren't to be mocked; they were to be admired.

I realize now that this happened because competition is different today than it was just a few decades ago. Businesses in general are moving much faster, and ideas can be replicated on the cheap. Competitors—and even companies not yet in your space—adapt and learn, finding ways to become better than you. And while they may falter, it's a much stronger bet to figure that they probably won't. Competitors are often smarter than you think, and if you turn a blind eye to them—or even blink for a moment—they're going to eat your lunch. If you care at all about the organization you're leading, gathering significant information about your competitors isn't useful. It's not something that might be worth your time. It's something you *must* do.

As Sun Tzu wisely advised, "If you know the enemy and know yourself, you need not fear the result of a hundred battles."

At Smarterer, a Google-backed startup I founded shortly after BzzAgent was acquired, we watched as Gild, a company that had been only tangentially related to us, deployed an almost-exact replica of our solution, which provided people a score based on how adept they were at things like Excel, PHP, and Photoshop.

While initial reactions included hand-wringing and disappointment at being counterfeited, we eventually settled on a valuable realization: there is no longer first-mover advantage. This has been replaced by an ability-to-adapt advantage. For those who are willing to gather as much information as possible, react, and innovate ahead of rapid market shifts, success will be inevitable. For those who fail to pay attention to everything happening around them, getting overtaken is the only possible outcome.

Yes, it's still true that if you have a good idea, at least ten other people are doing the same thing—but now they're watching you as closely as you should be watching them.

That doesn't necessarily make your competition the evil enemy. They exist for the very same reason you do, and in most cases rising tides do in fact lift all boats.

When it came time to sell BzzAgent, we had a number of direct competitors that became potential suitors solely because we had shared a beer at one point or worked together on authoring an ethical code for the industry. You might not end up as BFFs, but having a competitor as a "frenemy" can be incredibly valuable.

How do you get there? The route to a competitor relationship begins simply: pick up the phone and call them. Tweet at them. Don't wait; just do it. Actively seek out your competitors at a conference and introduce yourself. Let them know what you admire about them and offer to share an ingredient in your "secret sauce." Follow up and follow through. Send holiday cards; share client stories. This will break down the barriers that hamper your ability to learn from others and grow your business. The information you gather will be a critical asset that will help you stay ahead in your industry.

And if a frenemy asks, don't lie. You can say, "Yes, we do have copies of your proposals. Know what? I'll send you one of mine. After all, maybe we can learn something from one another."

WANTED: THE PERFECTLY PERFECT ANALYST

ORIGINALLY PUBLISHED APRIL 12, 2013

Background: 5+ years into the corporate workforce. Seeking a culture that won't feel like an acid bath.

Strategy: Fired up to go deep. You occasionally dream and often hallucinate about industry analysis. You wrote a book report on *Good to Great* before you were out of diapers.

Focus: What? Sorry, I was immersed in something.

Entrepreneurs: Their perspiration is your inspiration (you perspire only at the gym).

Conviction: Must have it, but without the jail time.

Badassery: Velvet gloves daintily tailored to fit your iron fists.

Writing: You pump out words like Corín Tellado with Hemingway's "For sale: baby shoes. Never worn." as your guiding light. If you write like Faulkner, we'll make you eat a keyboard.

Numbers: Quick, do this in your head: 1143 * $\sqrt{12}$ =

Financial analysis: You ride a spreadsheet to win the derby. P&Ls and PivotTables are snacks between coffee breaks.

Qualities: Smart, savvy, tenacious. Nice, but only on Tuesdays.

Humor: Relentless. Biting. Relative inability to be offended (except by Andy Dick).

Compensation: Money. Insane amounts of vacation. Tax-advantageous savings programs. Government-funded doctor's visits. Free rims for your new glasses.

Location: Boston. In the middle of a startup circus.

[This role was filled by the immensely talented Raphi Savitz, who did a whole lot more than analyze. I'm pretty sure Andy Dick wasn't offensive to him.]

10 WAYS TO STEP UP YOUR LEADERSHIP TODAY

ORIGINALLY PUBLISHED IN *INC.*, JUNE 31, 2013

Strong leadership is a lifelong pursuit that requires continuous evaluation and improvement. Every leader has her own style, and every company needs a personalized approach.

No matter who you are, or the type of organization you oversee, there are some universal truths. Here are ten of them:

1. **Don't try to get stuff done.** That's not your job. As CEO, your job is to enable others to execute effectively. A leader is the driver of strategy and vision; being caught in the weeds will only undermine the ability of everyone else to win.
2. **Forget about democracy.** You want to be a supportive, open-minded autocrat. If you make soft suggestions and constantly require validation, you create a lack of confidence among your teammates. Be assertive; lead by unwavering decisiveness.
3. **Never say "start small."** Seek out the big ideas and drive

your team to achieve them. If you start small, you succeed small.

4. **Make time your enemy.** The best CEOs move faster, get to scale sooner, and make things happen *now*. Impatience is a critical tool to motivate results.

5. **Tell exciting stories.** Having a vision and strong direction is only as good as how well you convince others to believe in what you're saying. Not much is as important as being able to relay (in person, on paper, Slacked, SMSed, etc.) stories that inspire others.

6. **Deliver finished materials.** Any document that feels raw and rushed will be perceived with poor judgment and won't be taken seriously. Pay close attention to typos, punctuation, page breaks, headers, and footers. Perfect formatting and proofreading are essential elements to sell your ideas.

7. **Prepare extensively for every meeting.** The more structure you can create as CEO, the more your team will know how to deliver results. You want to deliver crafted agendas and ensure team members feel accountable. Provide clear roles, clarify expectations in advance, and oversee meetings by deliberately pacing each section.

8. **Remove teammates who don't crush it. Immediately.** The only route to success is getting fantastic people to achieve greatness. The clichés are true: few get better at hiring; many get better at firing. Being one teammate down is better than having an underperformer bringing the whole team down.

9. **Lead by communicating.** To inspire a team, you should use the power of strong, clear communication. Silence results in complacency, so always (always!) respond and do so on your teammates', clients', or competitors' time. We live in an asynchronous world these days; finding synchronicity is a competitive advantage.

10. **Behave like your company is publicly traded.** What would you do if you knew that every decision you made would be visible to shareholders, affect share price, and put your career on the line? Operate from this perspective and your biggest ideas will rise to the forefront.

I'M TIRED OF HEARING ABOUT YOUR STARTUP DEPRESSION

ORIGINALLY PUBLISHED IN *STARTUP GRIND*, JULY 13, 2016

Startups are hard. That's a fact; no one is refuting it.

But lately it's become trendy to talk about just how hard they really are, and the toll they can have on individuals. There's talk of depression, and of the psychological price of entrepreneurship—and just how hard it is.

Call me callous, but know what? It's time to stop bitching.

Don't get me wrong, I feel for these folks. Depression is very real, and can happen to anyone. And if you feel it, I suggest telling someone, and getting counseling and medical help.

But we're talking about the specifics of *startup* pain here. I take a few issues with all of the moaning and groaning:

- **You chose startup life.** No one forced you to take the leap into the unknown. No one made you scrape together pennies to figure out if your wild, never-before-attempted, potentially batshit-crazy idea would work. You went to an accelerator or hung out at an incubator. You idolized all the cool companies like Lyft, Instagram, or Spotify. You wanted to be part of the community, and you sought to learn a new skill like growth marketing or engineering. You chose this.

- **You are privileged.** If you're in the startup ecosystem, it's likely you had every opportunity to graduate high school or college. Compared to the rest of the world, you grew up coddled. There's probably some capital luxury you're dealing with—certainly as it compares to 99 percent of the rest of America and certainly to third-world countries. You *are* the silver spoon.

- **You are working on challenging problems.** Because of your career choice, you get to use your brain. You aren't toiling away doing menial labor. You're not monitoring the fry-o-lator at some fast-food joint. You aren't stuffing envelopes or standing in the rain with a "40 percent discount for shoes today" sign on some street corner.

- **...with smart people.** All around you are people who want to win and are high achievers. You have every right to find a great boss or a company that believes in constant education. There is the opportunity to sponge during every interaction—to learn from those who have mastered their craft.

- **...who give a damn.** Ever worked at a company where no one cared at all? Where everyone just punched the clock and hated the idea of creating value or figuring it out? That is actually soul-draining. In the startup world, you are surrounded by people who are t-r-y-i-n-g. Who want to figure it out. Who generally help each other. Yep, they're imperfect—hell, they're full of flaws, egomaniacal, and somewhere on the spectrum—but they care enough to show up to make something happen.

I've run seven different startups, and yep, it's friggin' hard. I lose sleep, I stress about people issues, and I wonder if I'll ever be effective. I have massive imposter syndrome and I over-read tweet storms and books that sell stories of success—and marvel at how others seem to have it all figured out.

Yeah, I literally wonder if I am going crazy sometimes.

But I also am aware that I chose this. In exchange for the potential upside, I chose to deal with the ambiguousness and confusion that comes along with it. And if it gets too hard, I admit I am privileged and could choose to pursue another career path.

So, if startup life isn't really doing it for you, if you feel the always-on nature of the work is just too much or the pressure is too high, I bet you have a ton of opportunity to make a different career choice.

I'm OK if you want to write about it—it's therapeutic. But don't for a second pretend there's no way out.

The door is right over there, and there are a thousand other jobs you could be doing right now.

HOW TO BREAK UP
WITH EMPLOYEES

ORIGINALLY PUBLISHED IN *INC.*, NOVEMBER 2, 2011

To Kim N.: I'm sorry you were dismissed with anger and haste.

To David S.: I wish I'd told you that even though you worked with us just eighty-nine days, I don't regret that we gave it a try.

To Sam C.: I apologize for sending a signal that we didn't value every minute you were employed by us.

To David W.: I wish we'd thrown you a going-away party after you resigned, given all that you contributed to our business.

To countless others: I was a coward for having someone else deliver the news of your termination, and I wish I'd met with you directly before we parted ways.

After employing and saying farewell to hundreds of people over the past two decades, my list of apologies could go on forever. Yet one thing is certain: I never want to add anyone to this list again. And if you're in any type of leadership position, you should keep your apology list short too.

For most of my life as an entrepreneur, I got angry when employees resigned. I felt betrayed, broken up with. I seethed about losing a colleague who knew my complete strategy, my darkest fears, and my many weaknesses. How could they just take off, cast my company and me aside, and think about some new professional relationship to make work-love to?

When I felt rejected, I turned against departing employees. Early in the history of BzzAgent, my fourth startup, a key employee gave notice. I was bitter and frustrated and responded as many would: I started treating him like an outsider, re-crafted his image to the rest of the organization ("actually he wasn't great at..."), and began the process of working around him.

Within two weeks, the divide was huge; we exchanged half-hearted goodbyes, and he left with a shrug. Even though today we still share similar interests and are active in the same business communities, we don't have a relationship. Indeed, we hardly speak. *(To Kevin W.: I really valued those early days when you were one of the first-ever believers in our vision. Thanks for inspiring me way back when.)*

A "bad breakup" with an employee is a huge mistake. The one who leaves and the one who is left must both understand that the emotions at the time of departure—the frustration about mistakes that were made, the disagreements over strategy, and the heated debates—won't mean much as time passes.

Bad memories will fade. What always remains is a bond from shared experiences.

Shortly after the sale of BzzAgent, I tried to enlist my head of marketing to throw a BzzAgent alumni party, with the vision that we should have one last celebration with everyone who helped impact the business. He politely informed me that many people might not show up, as many remained disappointed and bitter about how they were treated when they departed.

"Many people might not show up," rang in my ears over and over. How could that be? We had so much fun working together.

Only then did I realize the depth of the ex-employee relationship chasm. I vowed then to handle departures differently. I decided to maintain bonds instead of breaking them, and it became clear to me that staying connected to former employees is more important now than ever. Here's why:

- **We are infinitely connected in a social world.** I founded BzzAgent as a word-of-mouth marketing company, but it took me ages to realize that word-of-mouth wasn't just our business practice—it was also a critical tenet of employee relations. LinkedIn, Instagram, Facebook, and other social networks ensure ex-employees' lives remain forever in focus. They'll be sought out for reference checks and—in the best cases—former colleagues may become future collaborators.
- **Former employees provide invaluable perspective.** They have critical knowledge about your business (and you) that practically guarantees candid evaluation—an external view that can serve as a complement to your own narrow perception. They can make introductions to clients. Their paycheck may not be determined by your vision anymore, but that doesn't mean they aren't an influence on whether your vision becomes a reality.

- **Monogamy in corporate America is dead.** We now live in an era where few will commit to a single corporate entity for decade-long stretches. Rather, it's common, and even expected, that people will change jobs and switch careers. Expect current employees to take part in side hustles or passion projects. Maybe they knit sweaters to sell on Etsy or are in a rock band. Maybe they advise other companies or joined a board. These roles only increase their experience, knowledge, and value.

Now, more than ever, departing employees should be treated with care and respect. When they leave, managers should thank them for their time and their contributions. In fact, a company's relationship with corporate alums should be fostered, beginning at the moment that you decide to stop working together, regardless of whose decision it is. *(To Kristen B.: early at BzzAgent, you helped us build a fantastic brand and I don't know if I expressed that enough!)*

Some very smart companies figured out the value of maintaining connections to former employees long ago. Open Market—one of Boston's highfliers in the late '90s—has an email list where alumni seek advice, share job openings, and create new relationships. Procter & Gamble famously hosts a big splashy event for their alumni every year. McKinsey & Company highlights post-McKinsey career and life accomplishments in their online alumni center.

It's even possible to maintain good relationships with employees you have to let go. In 2009, due to an evolving business model and economic depression, we had to do a round of layoffs at BzzAgent. We let go of two fabulous employees: Aaron C. and David E. Shortly thereafter, we provided free workspace in our office so they had a central location to work from during their job search. Another former employee, Rob T., decided he wanted to leave BzzAgent to start his own company. He launched it with a dozen employees inside BzzAgent's offices. For many years we cohabitated and generated infinite points of value through hallway dialogue; current BzzAgent employees were inspired that ex-employees were still considered part of the family.

Near the end of my tenure as BzzAgent's CEO, another key BzzAgent employee gave notice. But this time—with the historical knowledge in hand of nearly 300 employees coming and going—it was different.

First, I congratulated him on what would likely be an exciting career move and expressed how much I appreciated everything he did for us. We then worked together to craft a transition and company communication plan. And in the time between his notice and his exit, we didn't ostracize him— rather, we worked in unison to achieve the goals we'd laid out together. Ultimately, we threw a party and gifted him a bottle of Veuve Clicquot as a send-off. One might argue that, by the time he left, our relationship may have been stronger than during our time working together.

So, to Dave D.: thanks for everything you did for BzzAgent as our president for three years. I look forward to working alongside you again in some endeavor sometime, somewhere—and let's share a pint of Brown's Ale together at a future BzzAgent alumni party.

GOING BIG, GOING HOME, AND A $1.9M GUITAR

ORIGINALLY PUBLISHED IN *STARTUP GRIND*, JUNE 1, 2017

On May 30, 2017, Brian Halligan went big.

"Big" looks as follows: he purchased Jerry Garcia's famous "Wolf" guitar at auction for $1.9 million, with all proceeds going to Montgomery, Alabama–based Southern Poverty Law Center.

Let's get this out of the way: Halligan is a Deadhead's Deadhead.

He simply loves the music and everything it represents. He's studied the band's philosophies so deeply that he was able to utilize them as a basis for his book about inbound marketing. I've been to hundreds of shows and have met thousands of Deadheads and, truly, when I think of a Grateful Dead fan, Brian—all groovin', smilin', and singin'—is the first image that comes to mind.

If anyone should own Wolf, it should be Brian Halligan.

* * *

Somewhere around 2009 or 2010, I joined a CEO group that included Brian Halligan. These were the early days for his company, HubSpot, and he often exclaimed to the rest of the CEOs his mantra: "Go big or go home."

The group of CEOs gave him a lot of heat for that, partly because we were more risk-averse than he, but truth be told, probably more because of our own inferiority complexes.

And yet, his "go big" lesson to us eventually became evident: in the fall of 2014, HubSpot went public, generating tremendous returns for investors.

And while going public felt like the culmination of the dream, Halligan had a much bigger lesson for us in store.

That's because "going big" wasn't at all about taking your company public or making a boatload of money.

"Going big" is about being able to do the things that mean the most to you, to fulfill life's most fantastical dreams.

In one fell swoop, Brian donated a pile of cash to a great cause *and* is now the proud owner of one of his hero's most prized possessions. Simply put: Brian's purchase of Garcia's Wolf guitar is a reflection of the entire entrepreneurial journey.

If you can't do something like buy Wolf, then Halligan's right: you should *go home*.

* * *

Wolf was delivered to Jerry Garcia in May of 1973 by Doug Irwin—Garcia paid $1,500 for it. It had a 25.5-inch maple neck, a 24-fret ebony fingerboard, and a blonde western "quilted" maple body with a purpleheart (amaranth) core. And its inside was like a Strat, due to the installation of an Alembic Strato-blaster. It was first played in September 1973 during a private party for the Hells Angels in New York City.

In the fall of 1977, Garcia had Wolf modified by Doug Irwin (it apparently took two tumbles, one down a flight of thirteen stairs, during the first era). Wolf 2.0 had single coils and an effects loop. Also, Irwin removed the Wolf sticker Garcia had slapped on, and inlaid the Wolf name directly into the guitar.

Garcia played a number of other guitars through most of the 1980s, but eventually Wolf returned in the fall of 1989, when it was a guinea pig for MIDI synthesizer effects he was experimenting with. By 1990, it largely went back in its case—Wolf was last played by Garcia and the Grateful Dead in February 1993.

* * *

Since the acquisition of Wolf, Halligan continues to push the boundaries of the "go big" ethos. He's allowed numerous musicians—from JRAD's Tom Hamilton to My Morning Jacket's Jim James, and even John Mayer, Jerry's stand-in for the Grateful Dead's latest iteration, Dead & Company—to play Wolf during their live concerts. He's given new life to a historical instrument, ensuring the music never stops. Jerry would undoubtedly be proud.

If you're an entrepreneur of any sort, Halligan and Wolf should be a north star to guide you. In the song "Crazy Fingers," Garcia (with his lyrical wingman, Robert Hunter) offered this:

Midnight on a carousel ride

Reaching for the gold ring down inside

Never could reach

It just slips away, but I try

Yes, focus on "going big," but do it for the right reasons. Do it because the pot of gold at the end of the startup rainbow isn't really about the gold. It's about the ability to turn that pot into the gold ring you've always reached for.

Halligan reached for it. He went big.

And this time it didn't slip away.

YOU CAN BE AN ENTREPRENEUR—AND NOT GET DIVORCED

ORIGINALLY PUBLISHED IN *INC.*, OCTOBER 7, 2013

I have some significant but difficult news to share. After a decade of marriage, my wife and I have divorced. As with many divorced couples, the two of us never, ever thought we'd be here.

A critical factor in our decision was my evolution as an entrepreneur and a startup CEO, making me distant when I was on the road and distracted when at home. I must confess that, at times, I was more married to my job as CEO of BzzAgent and more committed to the startup community than I'd been to my wife, Beth. The two of us might have stayed together if I had known what to do to keep her from feeling like a "founder widow," as she puts it.

MARRIED TO YOUR STARTUP OR YOUR SPOUSE?

Let's face it. A focused entrepreneur is something like a drug addict: obsessive, aggressive, and focused intently on "scoring." For those with the startup "bug," everything from hatching the company, to building the team, to creating the first product is intoxicating, all-consuming, and fulfilling in a way that is difficult to describe. Thinking of anything else feels impossible. Wrong, even. The high of actually seeing your idea spring to life can be compared to only one other all-consuming experience: true love.

HOW IT ALL BEGAN

Back when my wife and I first met in the mid-90s, I was leaving a stable corporate job to try my hand at running my own show. Neither of us really understood what it meant to be part of a startup, but she said my ambition was intoxicating and she was proud of my drive to create something out of nothing.

Beth was a wonderful startup wife, mentally supporting me through a myriad of stressful moments like partner issues and negotiations that led to the sale of my first few businesses. I remember her partnership well: she once joined me on a last-minute trip from our home in Boston to New York to pay my respects to a coworker's father who had passed away. We spent countless hours discussing whether or not I should sell my first company and what I should do next. We planned trips together around my schedule. By the time BzzAgent was in full swing, I was happy and she was proud.

THE TRUTH ABOUT STARTUP MARRIAGE

But there were signs of cracks in our foundation. One day I called Beth on a speakerphone from the office and asked her to write a post for one of my experimental blog projects to articulate what it was like to be married to the CEO. She never liked being called on a speakerphone—especially with others in the room—and she didn't seem thrilled about being asked to write this telling piece.

Even so, she started writing and a few days later sent me the post. It detailed how difficult it was to be a copilot to someone who was glued to his BlackBerry (hey, BlackBerries were cool once), in the habit of leaving half-eaten pretzels all over the house (I forgot I was eating them), and constantly bemoaning "getting the barf-poop bug" on long flights. Yes, it ended with a touching note about my good qualities, but the impact of my thoughtless behavior on "us" was there. In writing. She was starting to doubt she wanted to be along for this nutty ride. Me? I wasn't willing to be different.

After the birth of our first child, I felt torn between the prioritization of family and the business. In *Home Game*, an autobiographical novel about being a new father, Michael Lewis writes that some fathers don't fall in love immediately with their children. He confided that it can take some time for love to happen and, for me, there was little doubt I fit that mold. In those first few months, my newborn was a fleshy bag of drool, a distraction who kept me up at night and made my wife a touch unhinged. Of course, I fell in love soon enough. But not before Beth asked me why I wasn't sacrificing work to spend more time managing our new child. Selfishly, I told her "I already have my baby." That was BzzAgent. That was work.

What a horrible thing to say.

WHEN STARTUP ADDICTION WORSENS

Our second child arrived in 2008, and the fractures were turning into a divide. There were now venture capital partners, a board of directors, and a full management team at BzzAgent. I had to be more attentive to the business than ever. Life-balance was impossible. When my wife said she wanted more help at home, I suggested we get a full-time nanny, and maybe even a chef for a few nights. She didn't want any of that. She wanted me to be there for her and for the kids. But I wanted to be in New York, San Francisco, and London. I wanted to feel the energy of structuring deals, creating new ideas, shaking hands, and making smiles.

And as I learned to become a better executive, the startup addiction only worsened. I started investing in other startups, advising friends, sitting on boards, and even launching new business ideas. Sure, we had the home with the white picket fence (green, actually) and the two kids in the yard, but inside, Beth and I were living separate lives. Yeah, we did our time in couples' therapy, and that served as a Band-Aid for some of this, but the truth became evident: I wanted to build companies and my wife wanted to build a family.

HOW TO AVOID STARTUP-INDUCED DIVORCE

I've had some time to dwell on the reasons my marriage failed and what I might have done differently. I haven't figured everything out, but if you are trying to balance being an entrepreneur with family, here are some things to consider:

1. CHOOSE A PARTNER WHO WANTS TO LIVE THE STARTUP LIFESTYLE

This is easier said than done. When love is young, life promises to be as simple and blissful as it is during the courtship period. But if you can have any deep discussions before you officially commit, it should be whether you're both ready for this roller-coaster ride of entrepreneurship.

More to the point, I've come to the following conclusion: a startup-oriented individual should be with one of two types of spouses. Either someone who is another startup-oriented person who gets the workaholic lifestyle, understands the importance of evening events (that look like parties but, I swear, aren't), and rolls with the rowboat-in-the-middle-of-the-ocean emotional swells of a business that is changing every day. The alternative is a spouse who will be utterly—almost to a fault—acquiescent to the needs of the entrepreneur. That means he or she is completely understanding when you're rarely home, flexible when schedules shift suddenly, support-ive when you're forgetful, and accepting when you always have one eye on your phone. In short, this person would need to be a total saint.

In my case, my wife didn't sign up to be a startup executive's wife. I don't think either of us knew what that meant. She was too much her own woman to be totally deferential (and I loved her for that) but also didn't really "get" my insane drive to do more all the time. I wish we'd talked about that a lot more a lot earlier in our relationship.

2. TREAT YOUR SPOUSE LIKE A COPILOT

After choosing a partner who is ready for the ups and downs of entrepreneurship, it's important to communicate to a fault. Over time, there's a natural tendency to pull back on discus-sions about work. Perhaps you're worn out from talking about work all day. Or maybe your spouse would rather set her hair on fire than hear about who-said-what at the office. But this is a kiss of death, because if both of you aren't somewhat in it together, there's no way you can understand each other's points of view well enough to remain true partners. I wish I had spoken up more often and asked for Beth's input.

3. MAKE TIME FOR EACH OTHER—AND TIME JUST FOR YOURSELF

You need three things: dates, breaks, and help. Make a standing dinner date night and find the time to relax with each other at least once a week. Remember why you got married in the first place. Take breaks. Go on vacations and enjoy life without the distractions of kids and work. And get help from other people. As Michael Nortan notes in his book *Happy Money: The Science of Smarter Spending*, one of the shortest routes to being happy is to create time. The best way to do that is to obtain resources when you can: hire TaskRabbit to do odd jobs, use Caviar and Uber Eats to get food delivered, get an accountant, hire a nanny, and make free time to enjoy each other.

Also, a footnote on therapy: most couples only go when there's something disabling enough to need it. My suggestion is that therapy should become something consistent, that you find a couples' therapist to see at least once a quarter. Someone who helps you communicate even when it's hard. Someone who can be the canary in the coal mine to those tiny fractures that can turn into divides.

FROM FOUNDER WIFE TO WIDOW

Beth and I only did these things from time to time. And, eventually, we found ourselves at the end of this section of our highway. We'll be fine. We're still incredible friends, and we're moving forward as co-parents who have affection for each other and our kids. We still enjoy doing things as a family. As one friend recently remarked to us as our families enjoyed lunch together, "This is so *not* weird, it's weird."

Beth and I missed out on the opportunity to make a marriage that lasted forever. Looking back, I realize I could have nurtured our relationship and my company if I'd asked myself—and her—some tough questions early on. And then, if we'd decided to make the journey together, I should have tended to our marriage as carefully as I cared for my company.

The lesson here is simple: act now. Do the hard work on your relationship. If you treat it as importantly as your startup, your marriage will remain alive while your business thrives.

I SOLD MY GOOGLE-BACKED STARTUP FOR $75 MILLION—AND I'M SCARED TO DEATH

ORIGINALLY PUBLISHED IN *INC.*, NOVEMBER 20, 2014

Yesterday my startup, Smarterer, was acquired by Pluralsight—and I'm genuinely scared to death.

It's not because the acquisition isn't 100 percent the right outcome. Combining the visions of Smarterer and Pluralsight made our future nothing short of astronomical, and by being acquired we delivered an incredible financial return for Smarterer shareholders.

So, why am I so frightened?

Because we are entering the incredibly complex, insanely demanding, highest-likelihood-of-failure fourth trimester.

It's the stage of growing a company no one talks about because in the startup journey, after an acquisition, many consider the story complete. Reporters focus their energy on the next rocket ship, and investors go back to hunting other prey. Yet, for the company acquired, the journey continues to unfold, and actually, the most challenging mile lies ahead.

Two weeks after my last company, BzzAgent, was acquired, my president and I trotted off to visit our new owners. After some brief niceties, the key contact from the acquiring company grilled us about why we should expect him to deliver us any value.

There would be no new clients, no integration support. We were on our own.

We walked out stunned—weren't we supposed to be partners?

Our president calmly whispered between clenched teeth, "We have a major problem." Thirty days later, he quit.

Welcome to the fourth trimester.

The truth is, most founders build their businesses planning for three baby-perfect trimesters:

- The first trimester is startup lore: creating the seed of something out of nothing, building a team, seeking product-market fit, and most likely raising capital with partners who believe in the vision.
- The second trimester is growing a real business: clients are buying, the company is scaling, and money is flowing.
- The third trimester is the delivery: finding a buyer, developing a combined vision for the future, selling the company, and creating value for shareholders. Slap that baby on the butt and hear it gasp its first breath!

But in a startup, there are actually four trimesters. That's right, four.

The fourth trimester begins as your company is being acquired (even before the third trimester is complete) and is the act of combining two newly joined businesses together.

There are a number of reasons the fourth trimester is so darn hard:

- **Building for birth.** Many startups build toward a sale, not toward running efficiently after a sale. Investor dollars and employee options are often structured to deliver the business to an exit, without regard to what happens afterward.
- **Sandwich dynamics.** Let's say your culture is whole wheat bread, your product is ham, and your team is hot sauce. Well, your acquirer happens to be Wonder Bread, eggplant, and mayo. OK, now try to cram those two halves together and make it taste good.
- **Transaction over strategy.** When another company I founded was acquired, I called up the CEO on the day of the transaction and asked, "Now what?" He replied, "We've been spending so much time on the deal, I thought you were figuring out what to do now." All of the work we'd been doing was to get legal and financial terms in place for the acquisition, and we failed to focus on exactly what we were going to do together.
- **Love pecks.** Post-acquisition, your workload quadruples as employees, vendors, and contacts seek ways to connect. Each love peck deserves your attention, and while individually they are manageable, all together they add up to thousands of distractions from the core task at hand: inte-

grating and creating mutual value with your new parent company.

Smarterer is being acquired; we don't want twins. We want quintuplets. Given that, we worked for months pre-acquisition to prepare for the fourth trimester. We prepared a joint "playbook" to deliver results from day one, with a foundation of working principles. But building together began long before that.

BUILD TRANSPARENCY AND TRUST FROM DAY ONE

Aaron Skonnard (Pluralsight's CEO) and I first met at a conference on April 8, 2014, and by June we were talking about putting our businesses together during a private lunch in Boston. One rule we set early was to be completely open and transparent regarding our businesses—to show our true colors, warts and all, and what it would take to create value together. No games. As with any relationship, trust is the foundation upon which everything else can flourish.

DEVELOP "WORKING PRINCIPLES" BEFORE STRATEGY

Working principles define the "how" for the "what" you're going to build together. When one of my first businesses was acquired, we skipped over defining working principles, and our incredibly tight strategy actually delivered total chaos.

In this latest acquisition, the Smarterer and Pluralsight executive teams—before we even had a merger agreement to review—created clarity on our initial working principles.

EARNOUTS LEAD TO MISALIGNMENT (...AND ARE FOR WUSSIES)

Bankers often quip, "Earnouts—rarely earned, but always paid." This is largely true because the misalignment an earnout leads to often stymies results, and the acquired company fights (or sues) to get paid.

An earnout only delays the difficult discussion on value; in one of my previous acquisitions, we were back at the negotiating table within a year of acquisition. In the Pluralsight/Smarterer transaction, we agreed on the price after two calls, determined it was the responsibility of all of us to create value post acquisition, and never looked back (both sides could have tried to renegotiate further along, but see point number one).

PUT EMPLOYEES FIRST

Immediately after the deal was closed, executives from Pluralsight met individually with Smarterer employees to explain compensation, benefits, and any changes to their roles. As a benefit, Smarterer also provided an accountant to prepare each employee's personal taxes for 2014. And most importantly, Smarterer focused on ensuring the deal provided every single employee with financial return and the opportunity for major growth. There is nothing more vital than enabling a stress-free transaction for every single member of your team. Comfort leads to clarity, which leads to results.

No pregnancy expects to go into a fourth trimester—and it would certainly be a biological miracle if it did. But in the case of startups, it's best to prepare as if it's inevitable. Developing a playbook in advance, aligning on your principles, and considering the impact to each and every employee is the route to effective integration and long-term success.

And there's nothing scary about that.

WANTED: CREODONT (NON-CORPUSCULUS) CORP. DEV. DIRECTOR

ORIGINALLY PUBLISHED JUNE 2, 2015

Background: 8+ years of making it hap'n, cap'n. Consulting and analysis give you street cred; shaking your moneymaker gives you groove.

Storytelling: Capable of weaving a yarn so tight people will think you're wearing a knit sweater.

Dealmaking: Handshaking. Smile-making. Not faking. Occasionally listens to Drake...ing. Erm...

Deck baking: Few bullets, fewer words. No funny shapes (unless round is funny). Use clip art and we'll rip out your nose hair.

Qualities: Smart, savvy, tenacious. Gentle, but only during crepuscular hours.

Communications: Receiving an email from you is a literary honor. Your wit is wet and occasionally stirred.

Connections: On daily regimen of Prilosec due to over-ingesting introductions. Can find two needles in each haystack.

Compensation: Money. Unlimited vacay. Swiss healthcare policy. Free Tesla rides.

Location: Over lunch, on a plane, wherever there's a desk. Sometimes in Boston.

Do: Not. Be. Annoying.

[This position was filled by Jake Vago, who can talk his way out of a paper bag—and even then, his hair will be perfect.]

7 HARD-EARNED TIPS FOR RAISING STARTUP CAPITAL

ORIGINALLY PUBLISHED IN *STARTUP GRIND*, MARCH 21, 2016

When I first tried to raise money in 1998 for a company called 360merch, a handful of plucky angel investors agreed to trust me with one million of their dollars. I wore my fingers to the bone in that business, hawking lenticular stickers and logoed baby-doll T-shirts using affinity marketing models—and then promptly lost the company all of their money when the internet bubble burst.

The next time I tried, for BzzAgent, nearly 200 investors told us to go screw off. Most thought using real people to generate word of mouth about products and services was a generally dumb idea (this was a pre-digital, pre-social world, after all), so we had to build the company to nearly $3 million in revenue before anyone would give us a dime. We went on to raise $14 million from General Catalyst and Flybridge Capital Partners—and returned $60 million to investors in eleven years.

My next attempt was with Smarterer, and I now had the

perception of success on my side plus a deeper network of contacts to pull from. It took us about 160 days to raise $1.2 million from Google Ventures, True Ventures, and Boston Seed Capital. In three different rounds, we raised a total of $4 million. Turns out that was a pretty solid bet, and we returned $75 million to investors in just under four years (which eventually skyrocketed to $150 million due to Pluralsight's eventual public offering).

Shortly after leaving Pluralsight, I raised capital for a new startup, Mylestone. The $1.5 million raise was incredibly swift and awfully quiet—fifty-six days from start to finish.

Venture fundraising is a funny thing. It's a sophisticated game with teams and rules and failures and victories. There's a lot of skill, sure, but much more luck. All sorts of things can impact a raise: the idea, the team, market conditions, fund dynamics, competing raises.

Hell, even the damn weather has an effect.

Each fundraise is like creating a painting: experience doesn't make it any easier, but you're certainly better at knowing the aesthetic, the weight of the brush, and how much color to use. And—as evidenced by Mylestone's first venture raise— understanding which paint to lay down and when to splatter versus stroke certainly makes the art at the end nicer to look at. Here's how we made that particular painting, and the lessons along the way:

1. BE LOYAL

I started the raise by going directly to angels who had backed me before. Shikhar Ghosh and Guli Arshad have backed almost all of my companies—even the ones they didn't like (beauty is in the eye of the beholder, and generating repeat returns doesn't hurt). I went to them first. They're loyal to me; I'm loyal to them.

Next, I went to Mark Gerson and Scott Kurnit, NYC residents who are accomplished entrepreneurs of ridiculous caliber. Generous with their time and advice and friendship. Invaluable in Smarterer's success; loyalty comes first. With their commitments, I now had momentum to approach others.

2. DON'T BE DESPERATE

I'd made a number of angel investors fifteen times their money, and I reached out to the best of them next. You'd figure they'd be easy to land, but a few of them didn't bite to invest in this company. Why? Could be they're over-invested elsewhere, or their model of investing is changing, or their kid had the flu when I asked.

Or the damn weather again.

It doesn't really matter, but what does matter is I didn't push beyond the first request. If immediate interest wasn't apparent, I just moved on because—above all else—you can't look desperate. Desperation smells like weakness, and investors can smell it like horses can smell fear.

3. GET A BIG CHUNK EARLY

After a few solid angel commitments, it was time for a big whack of support. I find it much easier to get the first institutional capital with a few good angels in hand. Time for the big guns.

The lowest-hanging fruit was Boston Seed Capital. They backed Smarterer, and I happened to be a venture partner there. Plus, they're awesome. [*Author's note: me saying they're awesome is akin to me saying I'm awesome, which is only really awesome to them and me.*]

As the first institution, they played an even more critical role in validating the terms of the raise and agreeing to "lead." The first angels can show their support but can't really define the raise for others to join. Boston Seed committed. We had a lead, and now we were rolling.

4. BE LOCAL

I can't emphasize enough the importance of raising on your own soil. It's where you will spend twenty hours a day building over the next few years, and your investors will become your advocates, recruiters, connectors, future fundraisers—but mainly the blankie you cuddle in your darkest hours.

Jeff Glass, Jere Doyle, George Bell, Joe Caruso, and Larry Silverstein are all exceptional Boston-based investors. They had priority over investors in other cities because I knew they could deliver, but also because an entrepreneur has to own their home court.

Deborah Quazzo is based in Chicago. But, well, she's Deborah Quazzo and she's brilliant and unstoppable. I'd be traveling to Chicago often, so I could pretend it was local.

5. HAVE A FIRM PLAN YOU WON'T CHANGE—AND THEN BE FLEXIBLE

I started with a cute little plan to spread the love and raise $750,000 in fifteen $50,000 increments. I'd focus on seed funds and angels only (no large VCs), with an uncapped note at a whopping 40 percent discount—double the standard rate. Beyond my rationale that the unheard-of 40 percent discount would compound the potential return, I fed off of the curiosity about the unique structure and fanned those flames: by getting investors thinking, and by making something original, I opened the door to dialogue.

The important part, though, wasn't so much the terms, but that there was a clear, crisp, unwavering plan.

Screw *"I'm waiting for someone to set the terms,"* which many entrepreneurs fall back on during a raise. Lay out your terms and then qualify them with logic.

Unique terms in hand, the $750,000 was fully committed. We were done; that was that.

Then things started to evolve. A few more investors—many in my gang of loyals—wanted in. Raise money when you don't need it, so I made $250,000 more available and increased the cap of the round to $1 million.

A few more checks and our raise was complete. It was a pretty little painting.

Then David Frankel from Founder Collective showed up. I'd been dying to work with Founder Collective for ages.

They were local and smart as hell. David's reputation was outstanding.

Founder Collective's DNA completely fit the company and the round, and I believed their involvement would be valuable for the next round (see point seven). But, Houston, we had a problem. They didn't like the uncapped note.

There are times in a raise when you bend, and this was one of them.

With a pledge to work through and have flexibility on all sides, we reconfigured the terms and then started calling all of the previously committed investors. A few had already wired money under the previous terms, but with apologies and hat in hand—and clearly articulating the rationale for switching—everyone agreed to the new structure.

Boston Seed remained flexible as well (they actually upped their investment as the round progressed), Converge and the wonderful Maia Heymann added a little to the pot, and now we were at $1.5 million total.

6. CLOSE THE CRAP OUT OF IT

This is where many entrepreneurs tend to flail, but it has to be a core strength. Forget "always be closing"—the refrain from Alec Baldwin's cutthroat sales leader in 1992's *Glengarry Glen Ross*—and focus on "knowing when to close" (guessing this won't catch on because I'm not Alec Baldwin, there are no Cadillacs or steak knives, and KWTC is not nearly as memorable as ABC).

Nothing good can happen between commitment and signature so, above all else, you must always, always, always move fast and as nimbly as possible to get to close.

I set a date two weeks out and emailed every investor clear instructions regarding what they had to do to "confirm their spot."

I ensured there was pressure: without confirmation, others would take the spot. *This was true. Never, ever lie while raising capital (or elsewhere for that matter).* I created a sense of responsibility and warned that they may be the only investor to hold up the close.

Then I pushed my legal team to update the funding documents and uploaded everything for fifth-grader-simple online signature via DocuSign. If anyone didn't seem responsive within twelve hours, I called them.

Damn it, people. Use the phone to close!

7. PLANT THE SEEDS FOR THE NEXT RAISE

All throughout the fundraising process, I met with a number of non-seed-stage venture capitalists. They weren't appropriate to fund the business at this stage, but don't forget that most raises begin long before you start raising—and this was a key moment to start building relationships with later-stage investors.

Bonus: venture capitalists—for the most part—are incredibly smart and experienced, and are a honeypot of competitive and market intel and advice. Even in small raises, be willing to meet with later-stage venture capitalists. Consider the outcome: free guidance from palm readers who happen to have lots of money at their disposal.

But be careful—if any of those larger VC meetings start to feel like pitches ("I'm going to have a few other folks join us" or "do you want to send over the deck in advance" are signals of this), back out. Don't confuse this as a time to pitch; the likely result would be poor.

Sometimes you'll make mistakes. I ended up in one "non-raise" meeting that evolved into a pitch. The VC called me later to tell me they were passing on an investment.

"But I wasn't asking for an investment," I stammered.

The dreaded "no" without even asking for a yes.

* * *

All in all, I was super proud of the initial Mylestone raise, but not because we managed to get it closed. I was proud because it's my damn job.

Fundraising isn't a one-dimensional equation, and during the whole raise, I was also feeling the rush of building the vision and recruiting the Mylestone team.

People were quitting roles elsewhere; they were changing their livelihoods—and there's no way in hell I wasn't going to succeed for them. An entrepreneur's requirement is to capitalize the business, and you can't delegate that to anyone else.

So now we had $1.5 million to turn our vision into some form of a reality. *That equated to exactly seventy-eight weeks.*

Every week counted.

And you can sure as shit bet I knew exactly which of those weeks I'd fire up the fundraising engines again.

33 BOSTON-AREA CEOS AND THEIR DIFFERENCES

ORIGINALLY PUBLISHED IN *STARTUP GRIND*, MARCH 21, 2017

Here's a secret: every great startup CEO I know is weird.

OK, that may be harsh. Maybe *weird* isn't the right word. Maybe it's quirky. Or different. Or...unique.

Unique. Yeah, that's probably more like it.

Unique has a few indicators: living in a potential alternate reality, establishing his or her own rules, maximizing superpowers, and generating a distortion field that ensnares most people who end up in their vortex.

If harnessed right, these attributes are magnetic. They're what enables next-level startup CEOs to harness brilliant minds, to make those minds willing to follow them into battle; they're what enables them to enrapture venture capitalists into funding their ideas and what provides them the tenacity to create mountains out of molehills.

With that in mind, here's my running list of some of Boston's finest startup CEOs—and what makes each of them just a little bit...unique.

* * *

FRED SHILMOVER, INSIGHTSQUARED

He makes smart look stupid and is a Julian Edelman fanboy. And may be a robot.

BRIAN HALLIGAN, HUBSPOT

Funny, transparent, self-deprecating, and ridiculously effective at the Irish goodbye, the French exit, and ghosting.

KATIE RAE, THE ENGINE

The mama bear of Boston Tech: "can be cuddly and lovable but also has a ferocious side when it's necessary to protect her cubs."

BEN RUBIN, 10% HAPPIER

I'd definitely drop acid with him.

SETH PRIEBATSCH, LEVELUP[1]

Once Seth publicly noted *friends* were "caustic," "ephemeral," and "utilitarian." Clearly a genius. Time will tell if he's Howard Hughes or Albert Einstein.

---

1   LevelUp was acquired by GrubHub for $390 million.

NIRAJ SHAH, WAYFAIR

Well-liked by just about everyone, he appears unfazed by just about everything. He's a regular guy who may be regular. But I really don't know about that.

BRENT GRINNA, EVERTRUE

He'll tell tales of baling hay in Iowa, with a soft-spoken "aww shucks" attitude. But it's a schtick. He. Is. Not. A. Hick.

Unless hicks go to Brown and Harvard Business School.

Bonus: he's Gronk-ingly barrel-chested and dashingly good-looking.

JASON JACOBS, RUNKEEPER[2]

His thousand-yard stare will scare the bejeezus out of you. I swear I've seen Tweety Bird in his eyes.

DAVID CANCEL, DRIFT

Mysteriously cryptic and yet mind-numbingly straightforward. I'm 98 percent sure he hypnotized me once over lunch.

ART PAPAS, BULLHORN

Apparently, 80 percent of Americans fall short of the 3-to-1 positivity ratio. Not Art. He's constantly pinching himself about how fortunate he is. The guy is a walking double rainbow.

---

2   Runkeeper was acquired by ASICS for $85 million.

NICK RELLAS, DRIZLY[3]

Lou Diamond Philips (Jose Chavez y Chavez) in *Young Guns*. Possibly during the peyote ritual. No, now you stop it. Just because he founded a booze company doesn't mean he's Charlie Sheen.

MATT BARBA, PLACESTER

Young Guns II. Emilio Estevez. Probably wants to be Kiefer Sutherland, but who doesn't?

GRANT DEKEN, GRAPEVINE[4] AND UNSTACK

He's hella good at "Ganbei!" with Maotai (post nailing an investment from Chinese billionaire Bruno Wu). Witty and relentless, his moral compass is so strong it'll pull the change out of your pocket.

IRA HERNOWITZ, KINDARA[5]

A veteran of Hasbro and Stride Rite, he's new to the startup scene, so is in constant tofu mode. Bald and no BS, he's sharp as a tack and gives good meeting.

RALPH FOLZ, WORDSTREAM[6]

Calm, collected, and matter-of-factly fierce. Got a problem, he'll fix it. Just like *Pulp Fiction*'s the Wolf.

---

3   Rellas is no longer with Drizly.

4   Grapevine was acquired with undisclosed terms.

5   Kindara was acquired with undisclosed terms.

6   WordStream was acquired for $150 million.

JEFF GLASS, HOMETAP

A conversation with Jeff requires you to yank up your witty banter trunks. Word on the street is he's been spotted doing audio voiceovers for Crow T. Robot from *Mystery Science Theatre 3000*.

NICK FRANCIS, HELP SCOUT

His hair is banging. No, really it bangs. It may fuck; I don't know. Charming and introverted, his talent-recruiting acumen is matched only by his capacity to unemotionally punt underperformers and culture-clashers.

PHIL BEAUREGARD, BROTHERS ARTISANAL JERKY

Social is the sword he slices with swagger. I'm guessing it's the same sword that cut off his man bun.

JANET COMENOS, SPOTTED

She'll crush you in sales. She'll crush you in tennis. She'll crush the piano (and she'll probably crush the crush you have on her). If she's not first, best, or winning, she's not playing.

ROB MAY, TALLA[7]

I'm confident he is confident.

---

7   Rob May is the former CEO of Talla.

GREG SEGALL, ALYCE

The guy is so intense he makes double-the-caffeine High Voltage Bones coffee seem timid.

NICOLE STATA, BOSTON SEED CAPITAL

The hostess with the mostest, and damn good with a martini. She wields unmatched generosity with incredible finesse.

BEN CARCIO, PROMOBOXX[8]

Bluffs hard; has a serious poker face. Plays chicken like Kevin Bacon in *Footloose*.

JASON ROBINS, DRAFTKINGS

Spend thirty minutes with Robins and you'll swear he's generated a thousand-row Excel file on you, with calculations like TRIM(UPPER(MID(A1,3,2))).

PAUL ENGLISH, LOLA[9]

They say there are 114 spiritual power chakras in the human body. English's bold freneticism—he's practically dripping electricity—proves there's a 115th.

TJ PARKER, PILLPACK[10]

So understated, it's disarming. OK, he looks a little bit like Ed

---

8   Ben Carcio is no longer the CEO of Promoboxx, but is still on the board of directors.

9   Paul English is no longer the CEO of Lola, but is still on the board of directors.

10   PillPack was acquired by Amazon for $750 million.

Sheeran, so how would you feel, if the shape of you...saw the fire...on the castle on the hill?

RIC CALVILLO, NANIGANS

It's never a question of where you stand—it's his way or the highway. An incredibly talented, incredibly driven one-man army.

POLINA RAYGORODSKAYA, WANDERU

Direct, different, and indifferent. Apparently Wanderu is Russian for Wanderu.

JEFF IMMELT, GE[11]

Word is he liked to get into costume to "meet the people." Supposedly, he once sported Counting Crows' Adam Duritz-style dreadlocks on the corner near Boston's Lucky's Lounge.

ARIEL DIAZ, BLISSFULLY

Excuse me, sir, your collar is sticking out of your shirt.

What?

<awkward pause, subtle stammer>

No, really, your collar is sticking out of your shirt.

Oh, you were serious. OK.

---

11   Jeff Immelt is no longer the CEO of GE. But still loaded, clearly.

ROCHELLE NEMROW, FAMILYID

Funny, disarming, and tenacious. I check my wallet every time she passes me in a crowded bar.

VISHAL SUNAK, LINKSQUARES

Everyone's favorite wombat.

Herbivorous, crepuscular.

Cuddly, but muscular.

CHASE GARBARINO, HQO

Kind of like Paul Newman in *The Hustler*. Does that make co-founder Greg Gomer Jackie Gleason?

YOU ARE A CAT-MAULING PRODUCT MANAGER

ORIGINALLY PUBLISHED AUGUST 10, 2013

Seeking an insanely talented, overwhelmingly smart, absurdly likable, and appropriately egomaniacal senior product executive.

- You're so curious, you leave a trail of dead felines in your wake.
- Speaking of cats, if Usain Bolt miraculously had a child with a cheetah, you could beat it in the 100m.
- Your ability to yap code and rub antennae with engineers is so impressive, they'll show you their polyhedral d12 die.
- You can sell catnip to dogs and Snausages to cats.
- You're a *Passiflora edulis*. We like you plump for your size, with a wrinkly surface—and we don't give two squats about your membranous sacs.
- E.* N. T. J. (* I. equally loved.)
- You have the ability to solve problems like Rube Goldberg, you can draw a perfect circle, and your wireframes are geometric works of art.

- Data? You don't do anything without consulting Count Chocula.
- You are so gifted, we want to wrap you in a bow of cash and equity.

[This role was filled by the calm, cool, and collected Krishna Kannan. I'm not sure if he likes cats.]

HIRE A HEAD OF PRODUCT IN 11 STEPS

ORIGINALLY PUBLISHED IN *STARTUP GRIND*, APRIL 10, 2017

If you're anything like me, hiring for product is a complete and utter friggin' nightmare.

It's not because there is a dearth of talent, and it's not because product leadership isn't an absolute necessity for any startup.

It's because no discipline is as misunderstood, misapplied, mystified, misnamed, and mistaken as the product discipline.

April 10, 2017, was a big day for Mylestone. After a five-month search we welcomed Drew Condon as our new head of product. *[Author's note: thank dear God. I don't really pray, but if I did, someone certainly blessed us on this one.]*

It took eleven steps to bring him aboard. If you're new to hiring product leadership, these eleven steps can serve as an effective roadmap. If you have decades of experience, they can serve as a reminder. Rushing them won't do you any good—so get comfortable, buckle in, and let's take a drive.

* * *

1. LEARN WHAT PRODUCT IS—THEN LEARN IT AGAIN

What the hell is "product" anyway? This is a discipline that evolves so fast, even the experienced require continuous education. Check out the "What Is a Product Manager" Quora thread (https://www.quora.com/What-is-a-Product-Manager) as a good initial cheat sheet.

Finished reading? Good, now read fifty similar threads and articles.

Wash, rinse, repeat.

2. DECIDE THE MACRO

During their time at Runkeeper, Max Freiert and Drew Condon were apparently a "two-headed product monster." Max was the "business" guy, Drew the "design" guy.

They both led big chunks of the product—usually together and occasionally overlapping. I talked to a number of people at Runkeeper who explained it this way: *"Max was focused on how to generate value. Drew was focused on designing the experience, so consumers understood it."*

Before you get started, you have a macro question to answer: do you need someone to figure out the business proposition or someone to execute on the design so customers engage with that proposition?

Wanting "both" is a fair answer, but candidates will lean heavily one way or the other—so you should too.

3. CONSIDER THE FOUR FOUNDATIONS

Every product leader's skills are rooted in some foundation, based on early career history. These will translate into unfair advantages and how they'll execute for you. Here are the four most common foundations:

- **Engineer.** Will immediately win over your developers, due to their ability to grok and even read/write code. Hire here if you require more throughput from engineering or don't have a rock-solid CTO.
- **Creative.** Grew up illustrating, doodling, and designing and morphed into a human-computer interaction or UX expert, wound around the axle of the psychology of people, so this person will best help you understand your customer.
- **Marketer.** Wired to think about brand and drive audience using quantitative metrics; will measure twice and cut once. If you're already strong in engineering and creative, might be good to hire here.
- **Operator.** Likely began in client services or as a project manager—now exceptional at running Jira or Trello boards and breaking down tasks into tiny little pieces. If you need order out of chaos, this is the person for you.

4. SEEK ADVICE, SEND SCOTCH

Scour your network to find product experts willing to impart a little wisdom. Given they aren't interviewing for the job, their ability to advise and provide unfettered feedback is incredible.

"You're looking for a purple squirrel," advised Richard Banfield, the CEO of Fresh Tilled Soil, on the first of a handful of calls. Others who provided insights that narrowed the talent we looked at:

- Dan Ritz(enthaler) (Iora) shifted my thinking on how product leaders evolve.
- Stephen D. Rodger (Intrepid) whiteboarded the ebbs and flows of the product iteration process.
- Trapper Markelz (MeYou Health) offered insights into our model and provided superb clarity on candidate reputations.
- Brady Bonus (Mad*Pow) helped us define UX and provided feedback on every iteration of our product over the last year.

Banfield was right, by the way, and anything more than three calls requires a scotch delivery.

5. IDENTIFY "TALENT LOOK-ALIKES"

Yeah, you're going to plunder LinkedIn to connect with candidates in your network. But when that well runs dry, then what? Here's a trick to finding a slew of people you might otherwise overlook:

- Find the most talented product people you know. Think David Cancel, Sean Duhame, Grant Halsey, Joshua Porter, or Christopher O'Donnel.
- Look at their LinkedIn or Dribbble or Upwork profiles to figure out how they describe what they do.
- Use their descriptions to search for talent "look-alikes," or people who use similar keywords in their bios or describe themselves the same way.

6. DON'T GET FLUMMOXED BY TITLES

You. Product people. Get your stories straight. What's with all the mixmaster-grandflash-mashing of your damn titles?

Case in point: UX designers now seem to be called product designers.

So, are you a product person or a designer?

Oh wait, product is design now?

What's that—you're an "experience" designer, but not a "visual" designer?

OK, so I want a product designer, but not a visual designer, but one that has UX capabilities?

Forget hiring by title. Begin with this question: "So, what exactly do you do?" Then...

- Write a position description that's directional, even if not quite right. We chose product designer, because we wanted to attract design-oriented talent, but interviewed across all disciplines.
- "Deal with it." That's how one of our advisors put it. Hint: just ignore the titles, decide the macro, pick your foundation, and talk to as many people as you can.

7. NINETY MINUTES. NO MORE, NO LESS

After a candidate has met a few team members—and you've qualified chemistry—it's time to dive deeper.

Outline a specific challenge, and have the candidate lead a group strategy session as if they already had the job.

Make it ninety minutes—long enough to go deep, but short enough so they're constrained and have to manage the clock (that's how it is in real life, right?).

How candidates prepare for the sessions, how they gain the respect of the team, how they own the room—to quote Kenny Bania from *Seinfeld*, *"That's gold, Jerry, gold."*

8. BACK-CHANNEL EARLY AND OFTEN

Far too often, hiring managers wait until they're nearing the end of their search to back-channel references. Reputation is a huge indicator, and unlisted references will deliver in spades.

"Hey, confidentially, what's your take on Drew Condon?" is vague enough to ensure you don't expose that they might be looking.

Back-channeling early will allow you to punt the less-than-stellar candidates so you can focus your energy on the top candidates. You'll need the extra effort to close them anyway!

9. HYPNOTIZE THEM WITH TALENT

Once you are down to two candidates, it's time to call in your closers.

I leaned on the two most impressive product leaders I know: Jeff Veen (True Ventures, Typekit, Adobe) and Nate Walkingshaw (Pluralsight, Tanner Labs, Stryker). Both agreed to quick interviews with our final candidates.

Leaders of this caliber will provide unparalleled feedback (Veen's *"This candidate has a more contemporary approach,"* changed my entire thinking), but more importantly, the association alone will hypnotize candidates into wanting to "step up" to the business.

10. DECIDE WHEN TO PASS (AND WHY)

As with every single hire you make, do not accept anything less than what feels like a perfect fit.

If you feel unsettled.

If reference checks don't ask if they can join once you hire the candidate.

If people pause or caveat when you ask, "Would you work with them again?"

Then pass. Just do it. Even if you don't have a second choice.

Maybe this will help: an ineffective head of product will require at least six months of recovery.

11. HIRE DREW CONDON

Final tip.

But give us a few years with him first, OK?

THE 8-WEEK DANCE TO AN ACQUISITION

ORIGINALLY PUBLISHED JUNE 15, 2016

In June of 2016, Mylestone completed the acquisition of Heirloom. Here's the inside scoop on how many (smaller) acquisitions *actually* work:

PRIMPING [WEEK 1]

- Baboon-level Google search uncovers Heirloom photo-capture app.
- Mylestone team Slack-discusses (even though they sit elbow-to-elbow).

CUE MUSIC [WEEKS 2–3]

- Balter tweets at Heirloom CEO @ericowski. Response: "@davebalter would love to connect. will send you message on LinkedIn to coordinate."
- Cut to meeting at a hipster coffee shop in San Francisco*. Turns out, Heirloom is currently evaluating dance partners.
- Mylestone team confirms strategy over whiteboard sessions with annoyingly half-dry markers.

COMMENCE TWERKING [WEEKS 4–7]

- Phone call from Balter to Owski to ask for the next dance.
- Slow waltz over a few weeks to align on overall deal structure.
- Legal duet ensues, basically coordinated synchronization to formalize paperwork.
- Last call snuggle-bunny slow dance includes final price and approval from stakeholders.

THE KISS GOODNIGHT [WEEKS 8+]

- Their eyes lock. Signature.
- Balter and co-founding Owski brothers celebrate over a sweet dinner at San Francisco Gin & Tapas joint**.
- Executing on post-transaction items begins. Balter expects non-malicious surprises and triple the work planned.

@google, @slack, @linkedin, and @twitter make appearances courtesy of Silicon Valley.

Email on loan from Ray Tomlinson. Phone procured from Alexander Graham Bell. Whiteboard appeared as understudy for @ ideapaint.

*Sightglass Coffee

**Aatxe

Business Insider wasn't in the dancing mood. Cue the mainstream rewrite in the following chapter.

THE 5 STEPS OF DEALMAKING YOU CAN'T IGNORE WHEN BUYING A COMPANY

ORIGINALLY PUBLISHED IN *BUSINESS INSIDER*, JUNE 15, 2016

In investment banking circles, it's common to hear an old adage, "deals aren't dead until they die three times." In short, the route to a successful acquisition is unlikely to be a straight or easy one.

And while many startup CEOs spend their days thinking about how to become acquired, that path is usually marked by the need to acquire someone else first. So it's in your best interest to become skilled at acquisition.

While there's no one way to acquire a company—it's part science and part art—there are themes, rules, and frameworks to follow.

Once you get beyond the "why" of an acquisition, it's the "how" that becomes the true test of strength.

In June 2016, Mylestone acquired Heirloom. Mylestone is in the business of memorializing deceased loved ones, and Heirloom's mobile app, which beautifully digitizes paper photos and offline artifacts, was a perfect complement.

The "why" should be obvious. The "how" is worth taking a closer look at.

RECOGNIZE OPPORTUNITY (WEEK 1)

While researching our industry, we stumbled across Heirloom. Mylestone was in the digital space, but physical artifacts—like photos in old albums or picture frames—are often a key asset for remembering someone special. We began thinking about what would happen if we could leverage a tool like Heirloom to accelerate a user's ability to gather photos.

LESSONS

1. Acquisitions are often opportunistic versus intentional; strategies may be half-formed (at best) at the time of initial discussions.
2. Seek out and pay attention to adjacent businesses, not just competitors.

ENGAGE THE CEO (WEEKS 2–3)

I reached out to Heirloom CEO, Eric Owski, through a cold tweet. After a quick phone call to get to know each other a bit and discuss each company's vision, we agreed to meet at a coffee shop in San Francisco.

LESSONS

1. Always reach out to as senior a contact as possible. An introduction is best, but social channels simplify cold connections.
2. The first conversation is to clear two major potential hurdles: a chemistry disconnect or a fast "no."
3. Meet face-to-face to build a relationship. Deals require trust to get completion.

ALIGN MOTIVATIONS (WEEKS 4–5)

After internal strategy sessions, I called Eric and stated Myle-stone's clear interest in acquiring Heirloom. I didn't sorta say we wanted to do it. I didn't use words like "partnership" or "merger." I just told him we wanted to acquire the company.

LESSONS

1. Be clear with buying signals. Communicate in person or via phone (save email for the operational stuff).
2. Both sides should understand motivations. This will aid deal negotiations downstream.
3. There's a lot of ego in acquisitions. The act of acquiring feels powerful, and the act of being acquired (often) gives the impression of success.

BRING IN THE LAWYERS (WEEKS 6–7)

Eric and I discussed price a bit, but didn't settle on anything; it was merely to gauge expectations on both sides.

Concurrently, our teams were working on how we might align toolsets. Lawyers began drafting acquisition documents and we kicked off due diligence—the act of gathering details about business operations—to evaluate and appraise the business.

LESSONS

1. Delay finalizing price as long as possible. Resource allocation and momentum often make it hard to turn back.
2. Utilize appreciation, anger, fear, and compassion wisely. Emotions are a strong negotiating tool.
3. The pace of the transaction will be set entirely by financial and legal diligence.

CLOSE THE DEAL (WEEKS 8+)

Each side redlined the legal agreement, and after some quick dialogue we compromised to full alignment. We set a deadline for closing (the day the deal would be complete), and documents were passed back and forth for signatures.

LESSONS

1. Create a clear close date, as deals often drag on during the last mile.
2. Prepare for three times the work and a few surprises post signature (integration is often much harder than dealmaking).
3. Always have a closing dinner. The relationship is just getting started!

THE FRIDAY BEFORE MEMORIAL DAY SUCKS

ORIGINALLY PUBLISHED IN *STARTUPS AND VENTURE CAPITAL*, MAY 26, 2017

Running a startup is a constant struggle of emotions.

One day you're seeing the forest through the trees, storming the castle, and making it happen. The next, you wonder if everything you're doing is half-baked, if you're making it all up (you probably are), and if you'll ever get the traction, revenue, or results you reflect on during your goddamn mindfulness sessions.

Which is why the Friday before Memorial Day sucks.

- Half your employees took the day off.
- Another 1/3 decide to "WFH" that morning (notifying the company via Slack, of course).
- Every customer, client, and partner is suddenly en route somewhere—yeah, they'll "pick up the conversation next week."

So you start doing all of the things you never have enough time to do. You set up your new computer. You fill out that bank paperwork. You walk to lunch. You look at financials. You wonder if you should write a *Medium* article.

You shoot the shit with the remaining 16 percent of employees who decided to come in. (Meanwhile, they're all wondering why they bothered coming in at all.)

The fact is, in a startup, every single day's mental state is derived specifically from the momentum you can feel all around you.

With a swirling wind of activity, you can be confident you're working toward something real. When that activity wavers, you're a fucking flat tire. You're a deflated balloon. A fool, a false prophet, an imposter.

The Tuesday after Memorial Day can never come fast enough.

ON TRUTH AND TRUE VENTURES

ORIGINALLY PUBLISHED MARCH 2, 2017

Back in 2006, Tony Conrad adjusted the scarf around his neck and strolled into the offices of BzzAgent. Tony was the CEO of Sphere, a blog syndication/search platform, and was looking to hire BzzAgent to accelerate adoption of their product. We eventually struck a deal, with one caveat from Tony: while he wasn't ready to run the program yet, he wanted to be sure a spot was reserved for him. The fee: $70,000.

A few weeks later, Sphere's 50 percent deposit check showed up in the mail. We cashed it, calendared a launch date, and focused on other things. As the launch date neared, we connected with Tony to begin development, but he demurred: he wasn't ready yet—they were continuing to refine Sphere's product—but he still wanted to make sure he had the slot. So we kicked the launch date out eight more weeks. That date came and went, and so did the slot we'd set for eight weeks after that.

Then, six months later, Tony's on the phone:

"Here's the easiest $70,000 you'll ever make," he says. "I'm not going to run a program with BzzAgent, but I'm cutting you a check for the remaining $35,000."

I (of course) refused the offer, but Tony wouldn't have it. Turns out Sphere had evolved from B2C to B2B, and a BzzAgent campaign would no longer fit with its objectives. That was his problem, not ours, he claimed.

We didn't do anything, I noted. We couldn't possibly accept his money. But Tony refused to allow us to let him off the hook—he argued that he knew we, as a startup, had likely already booked the sale, and the impact of us having to write off the booking would be unfavorable from a number of perspectives.

Round after round of back-and-forth like a dinner check—him offering, me resisting—and I finally gave in. A few weeks later the remaining $35,000 showed up in the mail.

I remember staring at the check with our COO. He turned to me and said,

"That Tony Conrad. What a mensch."

* * *

When other entrepreneurs ask me why we raised capital from True Ventures (for Smarterer and Mylestone and Flipside Crypto...we're repeat offenders), there are a thousand answers that would easily quantify their value:

- The fairness with which they negotiate
- The ability to not sweat the small stuff

- The partner team dynamic
- The willingness to do actual work
- The founder community they create
- The respect of other venture capitalists

The list goes on and on.

But it's the "Tony Mensch" story that always pops into my head first. Not just because of Tony himself—yes, he's clearly an awesome guy with a strong moral compass—but because the behavior exemplifies everything you need to know about working with True Ventures.

The truth about True: they just get it.

* * *

Last October, I had the fortune of attending True Ventures Founder Camp in Carmel, California. Besides the draw of an idyllic location, Founder Camp is one of those events where you get to see a glimpse into the future. As dinner was wrapping, I watched two entrepreneurs show off the drones they were building. One lifted off poolside, while the other was dropped right into the pool, where it performed all sorts of wild aqua maneuvers. At the next table, Dhananja Jayalath (DJ), the CEO of Athos, was doing tricep dips, glute kickbacks, and mountain climbers—his clothes registering his every muscle movement to evaluate strength conditioning.

Having exited Smarterer in 2014, I wasn't attending as an active True CEO, but was on a panel about M&A to help other CEOs with their exits. The travel through Carmel was perfect, as I needed to be in California to finalize the terms of a different venture fund backing Mylestone.

Before my panel, I caught up with Tony. We discussed my impending pitch to the other fund, which naturally kicked off a dialogue on whether this was a potential investment for True. I wanted to be very careful here: the other venture investor had shown interest but was not committed, and Mylestone hadn't found product-market fit. To be honest, we were doing a drunkard's walk trying to find where product could fit our vision. I certainly didn't want to represent that we were something we were not.

Tony suggested I run the Mylestone idea by Jon Callaghan, who co-founded True. I'd known Jon a bit from the Smarterer days, but had never really gone deep with him, so when we first sat down to discuss Mylestone, I didn't really know what to expect.

More than anything, I was fearful that he would see through the business—we had strong conviction and believed in where we were headed, but our metrics and results were meager at best. Was he going to think Mylestone was just smoke and mirrors?

As the event was wrapping, Jon and I found a small table near a cold firepit, and I launched into my pitch, which was centered around memorializing the deceased. Jon listened closely, and then a funny thing happened. He didn't try to poke holes in our vision. He didn't ask about market size. He didn't try to compare us to another company.

He started connecting.

He spoke to his passion for capturing memories, how he is a rabid "journaler," how he's been trying to find a good way to preserve his lifetime memories and make them infinitely shareable.

One might argue we were actually at odds with each other's worldviews. Mylestone was focused on *memorializing death*, whereas Jon was passionate about *memorializing life*. Many VCs might have concluded that we were on the wrong path, pushed their own opinion, and passed because our vision didn't equate to theirs. But Jon didn't try to sway me that focusing on "death" was incorrect; rather, he drew conclusions and connected on a level above that: *memories were important, in both life and death.*

Mylestone was nothing short of imperfect. It was nascent, amoeba-like. Raw. You could poke holes in it from every direction. But Jon didn't do that. He wanted to see what could be possible. To see the story behind the story. Jon wanted to let the idea breathe.

True. They get it.

* * *

Back in 2014, just after Smarterer's acquisition completed, Christiaan Vorkink from True called with disappointing news. Christiaan had spent some time on the Smarterer board of directors, was an investing partner, and also operationalized the systems that supported the True founders.

After some pleasantries, Christiaan came out with it. "Unfortunately, given you're no longer an active True CEO, we will have to take you off the founder email list."

You'd imagine that after successfully exiting a company, nothing could be less important. But this hit like a thunderbolt. The True founder email list was a place where you connected with the best of the best. Other True founders, all on similar journeys to create something out of nothing, asked questions, received answers, and supported each other. It didn't matter the type of business you were in. You were part of the family.

I played it cool, swallowed hard, and told Christiaan it wasn't a problem. I understood. But it was clear he heard my voice crack.

"Don't worry," he said. "When we fund your next company, we'll add you back on the list." At the time I figured he was just trying to be kind and wanted to fill the space with something that sounded positive.

On January 18, 2017, Tony sent an email to the True founders list: "I'd like to welcome back Dave Balter, Mylestone founder, to our founders list." More than thirty True founders replied, welcoming me back—Christiaan noted I was the twenty-second founder they'd backed more than once.

This was True. They get it.

MEN'S SKI TRIP GROCERY LIST

ORIGINALLY PUBLISHED JANUARY 30, 2019

- 8 boxes of Cheez-Its
- 4 bags of Ruffles BBQ potato chips
- 4 bags of sour cream and onion potato chips
- 2 dozen eggs
- 6 avocados
- Cheddar cheese
- Couple pounds of ham, provolone, and salami
- Gray Poupon mustard
- 3 bags of English muffins
- 4 sticks of butter
- 2 dozen bagels
- 2 boxes of cream cheese
- 3 bottles of Bloody Mary mix (Worcestershire sauce; horse radish; olives; and celery)
- 8 bags of ice
- 3 bottles of Grey Goose
- 1 bottle of Tito's
- 1 bottle of Grey Goose (yes, an additional bottle)
- 1 bottle of Jack Daniel's
- 1 bottle of Bacardi

- 1 bottle of Cuervo
- 4 bottles of Fireball
- 1 bottle of Baileys
- Coffee
- Milk
- Sugar
- 6 cases of beer (2 cases of Coors Light; 2 cases of Budweiser; and 2 cases of Stella)
- 2 cases of Coke
- 2 cases of ginger ale
- 8 cases of water
- 2 bottles of cranberry juice
- 2 bottles of orange juice
- 6 rolls of paper towels
- 2 bottles of Advil
- 10 frozen pizzas
- A dozen apples, oranges, and bananas; lettuce, carrots, and tomatoes *(Balter, is this enough fruit and vegetable for you?)*

Author's note: this unedited list is from an annual three-day "guy's ski trip." In advance, the group—a dozen normal, relatively intelligent entrepreneurs and investors in their forties and fifties—organized a grocery list. Yes, the result was apocalyptic on all digestive functions.

Also, it shouldn't go unsaid that, technically, it's "Cheez-It" not "Cheez-Its." Just like "moose," Cheez-It never has an extra S, people.

HOW WELL ARE YOU RUDDERING?

ORIGINALLY PUBLISHED IN *STARTUP GRIND*, MAY 23, 2017

Many years ago, I was a participant in a CEO group. One of the other CEOs was known for a hard-driving initiative that he claimed *ensured* results: every quarter—regardless of company performance—he fired one member of his executive team.

His rationale was simple. In a team of eight to ten executives in a fast-growing organization, people will invariably evolve out of their capacity. And complacency—by the team member who is no longer performing or by the CEO who isn't bringing in new thinking with enough pace—is a weakness.

The other CEOs in our group told him he was too harsh. We argued that individuals shouldn't operate in a state of fear, like some corporate version of *Lord of the Flies*.

That CEO? His led his company to a public offering, delivering great returns for investors and the employees—and, yes, even for option-holding ex-executives who had been dismissed.

* * *

Recently, I spent some time reference-checking a potential employee who had spent three years at a startup here in Boston. I back-channeled to a previous manager, who noted the candidate was effective but was always a little "off balance" during his tenure, and was unable to effectively use his skills—so they eventually parted ways.

His explanation: "Our CEO's hiring process was unplanned and ad hoc; he didn't really plan the hiring well, which was unfair to the company and the employee. Our CEO, he was just doing."

"Just doing."

Scary words.

Because that isn't leading at all.

* * *

Here's a fact: great leaders lead through a series of activities that define how the company operates and how the team behaves.

On the flip side, ineffective executives are often much less prescriptive. They fall into the trap of "just doing," responding as best they can to the pace and priority-juggling of the job.

Becoming an effective leader requires you to move beyond "just doing" to being prescriptive in your process and execution. You must reflect and direct each action and activity to generate returns.

It is often best to categorize actions into three specific buckets: Foundations, Constants, and Ruddering.

Don't get fooled into thinking each activity is on equal footing. Actions are often best delivered based on where they exist within your leadership cycle, which includes three distinct categories: Foundations, Constants, and Ruddering.

- **Foundations:** The processes you plan in advance, which become the basis by which you manage.
- **Constants:** Your personal unfair advantages that you deliver on every day.
- **Ruddering:** Your opportunity (and ability) to fix challenges as they arise.

A helpful leadership technique is to reflect on your actions and to evaluate them based on the category they exist within. Here's the cheat sheet:

* * *

Foundations are the big strategic activities that help the team know where they are going and why they are going there. These are most effective when they are scheduled, time-based activities.

Examples:

- Quarterly strategic planning sessions (OGSM, Playbooks, OKRs)
- Monthly financial results distribution
- Weekly one-on-one meetings with your team

* * *

Constants are your set of skills that you can 10× over anyone else in the business. As the leader, you can wield these in a way that can propel the business forward. There's no "right" set of constants, there are only the constants you are specifically built to execute.

Examples:

- If you're in product, you will create things: you might sketch or wireframe; you might manage Trello or Jira boards or gather troves of customer research.
- If you're in sales, you will sell things: you might review and update your pipeline or network, or "bang the phones" boiler-room style.
- You might be an excellent writer, so you publish often; or great at social, so you update often; or great with numbers, so you analyze deeply.

Long and short: use what you've got!

* * *

Ruddering is the filler to ensure your Foundations and Constants are effective. The importance of these cannot be overstated: how you rudder may very well be the difference-maker between a healthy company and a distressed one.

Fantastic leaders instinctually "feel" which parts of the organization require their attention. Their reaction-capacity is what allows them to put out fires and keep the team moving when they are stuck.

If done effectively, the best leaders straighten the rudder often.

Examples:

- Calling personnel meetings the minute you hear of team communication breakdowns
- Addressing infinite daily questions on strategy (e.g., Should we redo the home page? Which segments should we target? How should I close this deal?)
- When objectives are missed, reviewing key performance indicators (KPIs) and tying them back to specific activities
- Information distribution—about wins, losses, and changes to the business—to reduce confusion

* * *

So, how do you put this into practice?

If you're working to become the best leader possible, you'll consistently reflect on how you're executing on your Foundations, Constants, and Ruddering.

Here's a simple exercise I've found incredibly helpful:

- Go through your calendar over the last month and think about what you did each day.
- Categorize your meetings into one of these three buckets.
- Use the results to determine what you need to do more of, what you need to stop doing, and where you should delegate.

So, get to it—set your foundation, be consistent, and straighten that rudder. Your company will thank you for it.

THE ABILITY TO FLEX

ORIGINALLY PUBLISHED MARCH 25, 2019

Our driver is Russian. His English, a bit poor.

Apparently, he used to steer military vehicles in Siberia, which is comforting, given he's weaving in and out of cars, gripping piles of slush between the lanes, and squinting through near-blind visibility from horizontally pounding snow.

He drives a Subaru.

"If I didn't have you guys, I'd be doing 80 miles-per-hour, no problem. Subaru," he says, *"they no spin."*

And then he removes his hands from the wheel and twirls them around above his head, as if to prove the validity of his statement.

* * *

[Twenty-five minutes earlier]

We were frantically pacing the hotel lobby.

The tiny auto in the Lyft app hadn't moved for a good ten minutes. Headlight beams stuck, glowing pink. We called, frantic.

"I'm on my way," the driver confirmed. The evidence of fresh coffee on the dash when we finally slipped into the back seat suggested otherwise.

The doorman whistled inward, gazed at his watch, and bulged his eyes when we told him our flight time.

He put his fingertips in his vest pockets and returned to looking busy.

* * *

We woke that morning unrushed, lazy from a sleepless night of tequila and parchment-dry Salt Lake City air. I parka'd up and made my way to the front of the hotel for coffee. I scrolled emails.

Our flight was scheduled for 5:30 p.m., but having been on the road for three days, we were already thinking about home. We'd shaken all the hands, managed a few late nights, and made plenty of acquaintances at the conference (aka: boondoggle). We'd spent quality time with our good friend and host, who'd put us on the invite list.

We were already planning on skipping the day's carefully organized event (something about team competition; I could only imagine a potato-sack race) for another day of skiing: five inches of fresh powder from overnight and another six coming down throughout the day.

"Turns out there is a flight at 9:41 a.m.," she said, as if planting a seed.

The clock blinked 7:15 a.m.

Could we make it? It was forty-five minutes to the airport on a clear day without rush-hour traffic, but if we moved fast... maybe.

We deliberated for a hot minute, but we both knew how this would play out. The toothpaste was out of the tube.

Go time. We moved soundlessly. No questions, just action.

Rebooked the flights.

Talked our way into the ski lockers (*locked until 8 a.m.*, they said). Picked up the valet phone and bribed one of the valets (easy).

Realized ski tube was missing (add on another twenty minutes of going from storage locker to storage locker with the white-gloved doorman, hair permanently creased).

Packed all ski gear into the boot bag, strapped skis together, finagled into tube, and peeled and zip-tied FedEx labels.

Shoved overpacked clothes—originally shipped out for travel ease—into return box and dialed concierge. He was clearly refusing to answer the phone at 7:42 a.m.

Repacked carry-on suitcase. Scanned room for power cords. Chugged water.

Rolled bags toward the front desk.

7:49 a.m.

Opened Lyft app. Softly hyperventilated with the realization that all ride-share drivers were at least twenty minutes out. Down the mountain. In a snowstorm.

Began to pace in lobby.

* * *

People often speak of two types of skills.

There are *capability skills*, which intertwine tools with expertise: Excel and math; Salesforce and operations; *Medium* and short-form writing.

Then there are the *soft skills*: networking, communicating, leadership, and negotiation.

But there's another type of skill that doesn't quite fit either bucket. It comes from years of navigating a fast-paced startup lifestyle and being exposed to a myriad of motivated entrepreneurs, refined through the practice of accepting any task and not tolerating anything short of a solution.

The best of the best can do this on complete autopilot. They deliver like a far-fetched Rube Goldberg machine: one seemingly disconnected action leading to a solution for the next.

It's a defining capability that separates great talent from exceptional talent.

It's the *ability to flex*.

The *ability to flex* is the capacity, experience, and willingness to motivate, adjust, maneuver, adapt, and deliver on a dime.

It requires knowing who to call and when. What app to open. Which bellman to pry. How to manage luggage (never, ever check bags). How to reduce wasted time (don't check out, just leave the hotel). When to throw a fit (when they say all rooms are booked, which they never, ever are), when to demand the manager, and when to sweet-talk them about their name pinned on their lapel.

(*"Maebh, what a great name—how do you pronounce that?"* Turns out it's pronounced *may + v* by the Irish and means "she who intoxicates.")

The *ability to flex* is the ability to thrive in constant fluidity.

It's the unlisted skill that can turn a week of pain—landing at midnight with first meetings at the crack of dawn the next day—into breathing room needed for the important things. It's doubling down on deliverables by hitting the day flight, smashing four and a half hours of proposals, presentations, and financial models, and then landing in time for the mental respite of a home-cooked dinner.

The *ability to flex* is one of the most important arrows you can have in your quiver.

It's a skill that, if honed, evolves into pure art.

✳ ✳ ✳

The Lyft was now disastrously late, and we watched another couple swing their luggage into their pre-ordered XL limo service. We quickly discussed offering to stow away in the back and pay for their ride. Flexing by partaking in someone else's thoughtful pre-planning.

A conference call at 8 a.m. would change their ride and probably ruin their day. "Remember those people who..." they'd begin telling the story at some dinner party.

There's a difference between being capable and being rude.

We bailed. And continued to wait.

* * *

Our Russian pal drives up to the airport at 9:02 a.m. We're old comrades now. He says we're in good shape.

"Weather in Utah, they always leave little extra to board door close."

(Salt Lake is a pro-style winter airport, not so much Boston's Logan).

We sprint inside and note TSA PreCheck's long, windy line; we flex, double our odds, and split up, one of us heading into the CLEAR line.

Skip in front of the old guy taking his sweet-ass time arranging luggage into OCD-perfect squares on the security belt. Remind the daydreamer to push her bags into the screener.

The boarding door closes shortly after we settle into our seats.

Before takeoff, we send a thankful note to the event host and arrange to have a bottle of scotch waiting for him when he returns to his office.

We chuckle at each other.

The ability to flex solo is a rush.

Flexing as a pair? Oh, what a beautiful buzz.

OUR TEAM IS FUCKED AND SO IS YOURS

ORIGINALLY PUBLISHED IN *STARTUP GRIND*, OCTOBER 11, 2016

About a decade ago, in a private conference room of a Paris hotel, I sat silent as two grown men yelled business-oriented insults at each other. One of them—a bearded and bespectacled, seasoned and mostly soft-spoken executive—finally had enough and stormed out of the room.

As our team assembled the next morning, the executive quietly mentioned a family emergency that required him to return home to another country. Acknowledging nothing of the tension from the day before, he apologized to the nine other executives for missing the rest of our four-day offsite and exited.

Just another ordinary day as part of the highly dysfunctional executive team of a $1 billion revenue company.

* * *

Early in my career, I always thought everyone else had it figured out. While my team's dynamic might be unfortunate, others were operating with clarity, openness, communication, and efficiency. They knew the answers. They listened. They were respectful. They promoted each other's skills. They accepted failure. They challenged each other and loved it.

They—that company you always admired from afar—*they* were gods among men and women. They—the pedestal-quality, celebrity-like, media-worthy—*they* were out there.

But now that I've been part of dozens of teams, I've found that *they* are a myth. They are imaginary.

The truth: every team is a mess. Every team is totally fucked up. *They* are *all* dysfunctional in their own special way.

* * *

Let's talk about the team I led at Mylestone. Mylestone was a venture-backed startup comprised of eight people, and I happened to be the CEO. Here are a few things that we had to work through:

- **Silo behavior.** Making choices without involving others, thus creating "insiders" and "outsiders."
- **Communication breakdown.** Limited dialogue about what we're doing and when, leading to confusion.
- **Disrespect.** Ignoring communications, unintentionally or intentionally. Silence tends to cause frustration.
- **Role confusion.** Shifting priorities leads to overlapping roles, which leads to people feeling stepped on or on the sidelines.
- **Leadership.** A CEO (me) who finds it hard to trust can be snappy, and micromanages when he feels a lack of control.

Was I worried? Sure, I worried every day, but I refrained from being paralyzed. From everything I've experienced, this is entirely normal. *Every single team I've been on has had interpersonal issues and structural complexity.*

The truth is that coworkers are often like children on a playground: taunting each other, creating tribes and cliques, and choosing who gets to play and who doesn't. They operate out of confidence, pride, fear, and ego. Children or adults, no single human has perfected conflict-free interaction with others.

At larger companies—where executives were often deified as internal celebrities—some senior executives ascended due to political navigation and effective networking, not because they were more skilled or adept at working well with others. At one team I was on, a peer was secretly labelled the "Brown Crusader," because everything behind him turned to shit (and yet he was skilled at ensuring the mess wasn't attributed to him).

I can only imagine what they called me.

Startups aren't much better. In many cases individual contributors are thrust into positions as managers before they're ready. At one of my startups, tears were a common occurrence due to teammates talking behind each other's backs.

I'd argue that this is normal.

The fact is, a team isn't static. Rather, it's more like a wave in an ocean: sometimes rising to excellence—supportive, caring, delivering—and occasionally sinking to the bottom—confused, fraught, spent. At times *your* team may swallow a little water, but the key is to avoid drowning.

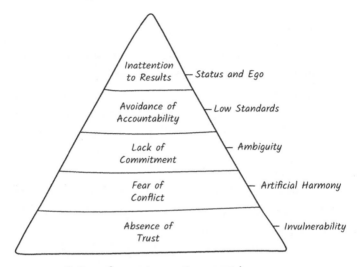

S Dysfunctions Pyramid

Patrick Lencioni's Five Dysfunctions Pyramid

In *The Five Dysfunctions of a Team*, Patrick Lencioni highlights fear of conflict as a key dysfunction resulting in "artificial harmony." On the surface everyone is smiling, but inside, things aren't so rosy. People aren't saying what they're really feeling, where they're blocked, and that handcuffs results.

My mom always said to me, "If you don't have something nice to say, then don't say anything at all."

Maybe Mom wasn't right about everything?

* * *

Ultimately, no matter what size, teams require constant, unrelenting attention; the team, for lack of a better way to put it, is a group of individuals who operate within the bounds that their interpersonal conflicts allow for. Limit those conflicts, and you become high-performing. Allow the conflicts to fester, and trust dissipates between individuals, greatly limiting your chance of success.

The net is, you need to maximize your team's capacity to perform *individually together*. There's no magic equation; I work on this every day. Here are three things that can help:

- **Be religious about one-on-ones.** Actual problems can be obfuscated by the team dynamic. Spending time in individual conversation, people issues become evident. If you're a manager, have one-on-ones. If you're an employee, ask for them and use them.
- **Don't let interpersonal issues fester.** Once you identify areas of friction, address them immediately. Talk to people. Try to get everyone to express their points of view and what would help them perform better. If you're a manager, help people talk to each other.
- **Have everyone read *The Five Dysfunctions of a Team*.** It's an easy read and a healthy tool for shining a light on bad behavior. Refer the team back to it when needed.

* * *

Nearly a decade ago, our COO, my teammate, sat across from me, stone-faced, after a combative internal meeting. Once everyone else had filed out of the room, he took a breath and asked me point blank,

"You know we're on the same team, right?"

I've found it useful to reflect on that reminder often. If you're on a team of any size, I hope you do too.

WANTED: ENGINEER WHO JAMS THE FIZZ IN YOUR BUZZ

ORIGINALLY PUBLISHED MARCH 24, 2016

- Aged 13-95. Male, female, or bat-eared fox.
- Puts Boudreaux's Butt Paste on ears to reduce headphone chafe from incessant coding.
- Realizes that the only nonreusable design patterns should be in the kitchen.
- Wants the sales team to cram "what-they-just-sold-that-we-don't-have" up their asses.
- Has quietly figured out a compression time-bending formula that provides 67.6 minutes for every daytime hour.
- Is often referred to as absurd, insane, paradoxical, and brave. Terrifies and confuses most normal humans.
- Is fully aware that one doesn't pet Rabbit or eat Celery.

- Will alpaca-spit in your face if asked to produce this:

```
{
public static void main(String[] args){
    for(int i = 1; i <= 100; i++){
        String test = "";
        test += (i % 3) == 0 ? "fizz" : "";
        test += (i % 5) == 0 ? "buzz" : "";
        System.out.println(!test.isEmpty() ? test : i);
    }
  }
}
```

Stack Stack City: Python, Flask, SQLAlchemy (ORM), Post-greSQL, RabbitMQ/Celery, Redis **** React > Flux > ES6 > Babel > Webpack **** TensorFlow, Numpy/Scipy *(Not lumpy Skippy. Stick to the creamy stuff.)*

We don't give two squats how many years or where you spent them. Just be better.

[I think this role was filled by Maritza Ebling, whose capability to code is only matched by her ferocity with knitting needles. That said, I can't be sure. If there ever was a befuddling era clouded by a healthy dose of repression, this was it.]

IT CAN'T GET ANY WORSE THAN SUCKING

ORIGINALLY PUBLISHED IN *STARTUP GRIND*, NOVEMBER 7, 2016

These days, it's rarefied air to witness someone sucking on a vacuum.

Phish drummer Jon Fishman shares that rarified air much less frequently in 2019 than he did in 1989. But when he does—as hard as this is to believe—it's actually something of a sonic treat: a three- to four-minute blast of guttural, gum-flapping vibrations, accentuated with thin-lipped, high-pitched whistling.

Somehow, with the rest of Phish vamping the tune behind him, it's completely in key.

If you'd witnessed the band earlier in their career, you'd know that Jon Fishman's vacuum sucking wasn't always so perfected. His Electrolux and his sucking alter ego, Henrietta, would appear frequently, about once a show, near the end of the second set.

Ironically, his vacuum sucking—it sucked.

But over time, Fishman began coaxing timbre and tones from the nozzle of the hose, sounds so unique that one of his vacuums now hangs on the wall in a Hard Rock Cafe.

* * *

If you're involved with startups or technology of any kind, you've probably heard this lean-startup call-to-arms from technology royalty Reid Hoffman: *"If you are not embarrassed by the first version of your product, you've probably launched too late."*

In October 2016, Mylestone released its first native mobile app. By all accounts, it really sucked.

And if you've ever created something out of nothing, something never before attempted (like Fishman's vacuum playing), you know the first iteration of what you built, in all likelihood, will suck too.

Every single company deals with this problem. It's not unique.

The manifestation of the process is consistent, regardless of the scale, scope, or sector of your organization—and that's just fine. Sucking isn't the problem; it's a symptom of how you get from nothing to something.

BEFORE THE SUCKING

- First, your team will say there isn't enough time to develop the product. Whether you give them one week, three weeks, or six months, it doesn't matter. It's not enough time.
- Partway through the build, at least one member of your

team will declare they don't know what they're building anymore.

- Urgency will be fleeting until you actually near the deadline. Attempting to push urgency earlier is akin to saying, "Beatings will continue until morale improves."
- Many members of your team will constantly try to stop the release. "It's not good enough!" they'll demand. Realizing they can't stop it, they'll fall back to a compromise of some sort of delay. (Hint: find an external deadline—an investor presentation, a big conference, or a press release—to hold the line.)
- Team breakdowns are likely at critical junctures. Some teammates will get energized. A few will pout. Occasionally, some will take their headphones off, say they've had enough, and walk out the door.

NOW THAT IT SUCKS

- You'll be embarrassed to show it to anyone. Demos will include sleight of hand. You'll instruct people to look over yonder, wanting them to imagine what it *could* look like *when* the next release is built.
- The marketing group will want to downshift from high gear into neutral: postponing major news, being quiet on social media, and generally trying to move the budget to the next major build.
- The sales team will complain. They'll highlight flaws and weaknesses and where the competitors have a better offering. They'll also bring back incredible market feedback, so listen closely.
- Fingers will get pointed. One person will keep muttering to themselves that you developed too fast.
- Meanwhile, even with all of the grumbling, you'll realize

that most people on your own team aren't even using the product.

SOLVING FOR THE SUCK

- You should, of course, urgently try to determine what isn't working and what you can do to fix it.
- You should take a long look at your development process—sprints, Scrum, whatever—and evaluate if you're building with the right goals in mind.
- Speaking of goals, you should ask yourself again and again: what are our core KPIs, and are we building to solve them? And, of course, your core KPIs should center on whether you're solving true customer pain.
- You should share your product. Yes, certainly with real users to gather more data, but also appropriately with investors, advisors, and partners. Why? Because progress is a great way to show value, and you can't get any worse than sucking. The next time you show them a product, it *will* be better and will demonstrate listening and learning.

A word of caution: don't lipstick the pig. It is what it is. Be transparent. Make a joke about it. There's no good story without a crisis, and this sucky version of your product may be the crisis you need. Someday you'll look back and wonder how you got so far.

So give your next product a shot. It could suck again.

Maybe it will suck less. But it certainly can't suck more.

And you can consider that a win.

17 THINGS A CEO DOES—WHEN NOT MICRODOSING

ORIGINALLY PUBLISHED IN *STARTUP GRIND*, MARCH 28, 2017

Recently, I self-administered some CEO therapy.

What I'd been told (by myself) is that a critique of my activities—nay, the opportunity to be subject to potential declarations of my ignorance, simplemindedness, and short-sightedness—would invariably aid me in becoming a better leader.

As part of my process—which may have appeared like awk-ward daydreaming or a microdose day—I realized the efforts of any leader are delivered in three distinct buckets: Founda-tions, Constants, and Ruddering.

So, as part of my therapeutic regimen (which I'd prescribed), I figured I'd document the results of my reflections.

While I'm vain and totally self-conscious, I tentatively hope it lets you judge my strengths and weaknesses.

My inside voice swears I can bear it.

* * *

Let's start with a few of the Foundations—the processes I plan in advance, which become the basis by which I manage—that are critical to producing a high-performing team:

1. **Develop the company playbook.** "Why do we exist?" and "How do we get there?" are more than existential debates. You can't bake the cake if you don't know the ingredients.
2. **Plan and lead strategic offsites.** Aim for once a quarter, but the rhythm is often dictated by major forks in the road, and when there are additions or subtractions to and from the team. People come and go, teams change, and a good offsite can recrystallize the group.
3. **Measure spending on a weekly basis.** "We have fourteen months of cash remaining" hides a basic fact: every single decision will impact how long you exist. Clarifying to "We have fifty-six weeks of cash to go, and next week will be fifty-five" enables the team to act with great consideration.
4. **Individualize management and mentorship.** Even when you chat dozens of times a day, weekly one-on-ones suss out the real dirt. Stay connected, help individuals know where to focus, and unblock anything standing in their way.
5. **Generate culture.** Culture doesn't happen on its own; it needs to be constantly massaged, managed, and maintained. Set and discuss values early and often; make sure there's something unique, freaky, or fun—and most importantly, teach the entire team to be accountable to one another.

With the Foundations set, now I can focus on the Constants—the personal unfair advantages I deliver on every day. Putting these on paper reminds me what I have to do tomorrow:

6. **Sell something.** Opening a deal is fun, but closing deals is thrilling. And no company starves when there are clients funding growth.
7. **Network with key partners.** Gotta kiss the ring. Especially when the hand it's on can feed you—or crush you.
8. **Connect with current investors.** You cannot "*get it and forget it.*" These people have a vested interest in your outcome; more importantly, the good ones will cheerlead when you're too far down—and tell you the truth when you're too far up.
9. **Raise capital.** You. Yes, you. You are raising capital right now. You just didn't know it.
10. **Engage the press.** They tell the story you can't. They're often friendly, but the majority aren't your friends—don't get confused by that.
11. **Write, right?** Putting it on paper makes it real. Tweeting partially counts. TikToking is just lazy.
12. **Fraternize with frenemies.** Rising tides lift all boats, so stop being so standoffish. Generate good will and karma will take care of itself.
13. **Recruit talent.** The entire team should be trained to attract and engage top talent, but at startup stage, obtaining the best has to be the CEO's job. And, for heaven's sake, make job posts fun.

Finally, I'll set the course with some strong Ruddering: my opportunity to fix challenges as they arise. Here are a few activities that unblock problems and set guideposts where they are needed:

14. **Set KPI reminder sessions.** Your team stumbles on a product update and the latest release doesn't align with KPIs. Pull the fire alarm and call an immediate team meeting to make sure everyone is aligned on objectives. This will happen only, say, a thousand more times over the course of your business.

15. **Answer daily questions on strategy.** "Should we redo the home page?" "How do we evaluate which segments to focus on?" "Why are there no forks?" Answer fast and often. Nothing kills momentum like individuals who are guessing.

16. **Massage the culture.** In an age of digital nomads with Slack as your core communication tool—and, hell, the rise of millennials—reinforcing "how we behave" with vigilance is the key to a high-performing team. *Rapidly extinguish any cultural flames before they become full-blown fires.*

17. **Manage the hire-to-start window.** *The time between hiring a new employee and the day they start is a magic window.* The team must be prepared for change. For the new hire: continue building the personal relationship and provide her a continuous flow of inspiration. For your team: activate them to build their own relationship, prepare them for any transition of management, and clarify how the new role will fit in with daily activities.

* * *

Now that my Constants, Foundations, and Ruddering are set, I realize it's time to take care of the body and mind:

+ 18. **Personally primp.** Get my 'do trimmed and teeth crowned—and cough for the doc once a year.

+ 19. **Microdose.** When not doing these things, read Ayelet Waldman's *A Really Good Day: How Microdosing Made a Mega Difference in my Mood, My Marriage, and My Life* or Michael Pollan's *How to Change Your Mind: What the New Science of Psychedelics Teaches Us About Consciousness, Dying, Addiction, Depression, and Transcendence*—and consider the delicate and magical nature of our brains.

FAILING, TO SUCCEED

ORIGINALLY PUBLISHED IN *STARTUP GRIND*, NOVEMBER 15, 2017

Here's one for you:

In October 2017, just nineteen months after launching the company, I officially transitioned out of the CEO role at Mylestone. I agreed to remain involved as chairman while Drew Condon, our amazing head of product, was aiming to take over the day-to-day reins.

Was this a failure?

Yes, it was. Yet it was the only way the company would have a chance to actually succeed.

* * *

About two decades ago, a guy I'll just call "Snake Eyes" (he was a bit weird and, well, his pupils were literally vertical slits, which gave him a reptilian vibe) was gushing about witnessing a rhythmic paradox delivered by Phish drummer Jon Fishman. Apparently, Fishman was going deeper and deeper into some syncopated pattern and eventually found himself stuck.

Snake Eyes argued, *"He just drummed himself into a corner, and had nowhere else to go. So he just stopped altogether."*

The story always baffled me—how could someone drum themselves into a corner? (If anyone has an explanation for this, I'm all ears.)

Regardless, Snake Eyes had articulated our exact feeling after the first year of Mylestone.

Our mission was bold: to transform how people memorialized their deceased loved ones. Fewer and fewer were memorializing in cemeteries—a socially and digitally transformed world magnified the ineffectiveness of paying our respects to the deceased. Our memories were captured in photographs, stories, and communications with those we loved. Especially as time marched on, when the memories began to fade and needed a way to be preserved. When we spoke to those in grief, or anyone who had lost anybody, it was clear we had identified a real and measurable pain.

Many people told us our proposition, no matter how valid, would be very hard to deliver. They argued that countless others had tried and failed before; that the empathetic nature of funeral directors wasn't enough to overcome the funeral industry's technophobia, and it was hard to ignore their incredibly low motivation for change (geographic proximity was enough of a competitive advantage for most funeral directors).

Our entrepreneurial bravado disagreed. So we got to work.

After a year of visiting 143 funeral homes, and about a dozen product iterations, we came to the conclusion that the funeral code was, indeed, too complex. In January 2017, we began focusing instead on the living: we connected people's digital photo libraries with a personal biography service.

It solved memorialization without the burden of grief.

People really, really liked it.

We had plenty of capital.

Our team was lights-out good.

But one thing was hard to ignore: overnight, we transformed from a business that sold to funeral homes (B2B) to one that sold directly to consumers (B2C).

The next eleven months became the most complex and unsettling of my startup career. The shoes never felt comfortable. Sure I was dancing, but it wasn't with any sort of grace.

balter

(bôl´ter) v.
To dance gracelessly, without particular art or skill, but perhaps with some enjoyment.

[MIDDLE ENGLISH]

The reason: in a consumer (B2C) business, my superpowers were on the sidelines. I'm really a B2B guy.

Of course, I set the vision. I managed the team. Worked on the culture. But underneath was the cold hard fact that I had no one to sell to.

No one to build a partnership with.

No one to B2B.

Our product team was focusing on customer interviews, willingness-to-pay discussions, and user experience roadmapping; our tech team was building the tools to operationalize the customers' needs. Our marketers were driving traffic. And I was finding myself more of a guiding light than a driving force.

A company must be wound around the CEO's specific skill. If it isn't, no matter the hustle, no matter the willingness, drive, focus, or creativity—it will always be less than enough.

Simply put, it was time for the company to be wound around another person's axle. So we wound it around Drew's.

Put your confidence and ego aside: knowing when to step aside is as important a skill as knowing when to lead. Here's to Drew as he pushes it into third gear and tries to climb that hill.

THE 20 SLIDES THAT RAISED $7 MILLION

ORIGINALLY PUBLISHED IN *HACKER NOON*, SEPTEMBER 24, 2019

Fundraising is a funny art.

It's a play in three parts: the Windup, the Execution, and the Close.

THE WINDUP

In the Windup, you're setting the stage. Rarely is a fundraise accomplished from a cold start with cold relationships, so a Windup often takes many months of getting to know venture capitalists and other investors. No pitching, no hunting. Just casual glad-handing, coffee meetings, and character-setting.

A good Windup will inform who you have chemistry with. *Nothing will happen without chemistry.*

In the final weeks of a Windup, you'll be laying some breadcrumbs. You'll be offering that you're *thinking* of a raise.

You're evaluating whether now is the right time.

Don't start if it isn't.

VCs are meeting masters, so if your Windup is strong, you'll be offered plenty of chances to meet and pitch. You'll reach out to anyone you haven't met during your early Windup to let them know that while you know a number of folks you might want to raise from, you're trying to get to know a few others—just to be sure you haven't missed anyone great. No VC likes to be left out.

In your Windup, you've been fastidiously refining your vision while generating indicators that there's a business to be polished. And your team has to be quality. Go ahead and get rid of that dead weight before you raise.

You're never *really* ready, so forget about that.

Momentum will tell you when it's time.

THE EXECUTION

Lace up, because good fundraises happen fast. And they can happen any time of year. Forget that crap about August being a bad time to raise. Do the rest right and the summer season becomes irrelevant.

You'll want to set up discussions with partners, not associates. Associates are awesome, but they're just one step further away from the truth. Principals are OK, just know you're going to have to have a few more meetings than you should.

Pitch live when you can. Pitching via video works too (Zoom finally made this work well enough). Don't pitch on a phone call. Always pitch with a deck. Pitch in an office, not a coffee shop. Pitch without random folks walking behind you all the time (no one cares about the hip vibe of your shared office space).

Decide on your pitch partners. If you can, pitch solo first and then bring in the big guns (e.g., CTO / head of data science at Flipside Crypto) for the second pitch once someone is hooked on the vision. This strategy saves your team's time and also saves something "new" for the second pitch.

Well-executed pitches are a series of stair steps, with each step allowing you to meet the next objective.

FUNDRAISE STAIR STEPS

- Hammer initial pitch meetings with as many investors as you like in two to three weeks. Find someone to lead (step up).

- Tell other investors you have a lead (step up).

- Find out what everyone else wants to invest and get people to commit to a spot (step up).

- Pit investors against each other to create pressure on close dates (step up).

Meet other investors throughout the process because you never know how momentum will change your story (nothing like a nearly closed round to excite new investors) or cause some to drop out.

Finally. Finally, finally, finally. Your deck will be critical. A few rules:

- **Make it memorable.** Venture capitalists see ridiculous amounts of decks. Help them remember yours. Slides should tell the story with *zero* voiceover. What you add in a pitch should be color. Speaking of color, get to know Unsplash and 500px, and your slides will do the work for you.
- **Fit the patterns.** Venture capitalists also have a shopping list they need to check off: team, model, traction, competitive landscape, TAM (total addressable market), and so on. Don't leave anything out. *And, Goddamn it, know how much you want to raise before you start.*
- **Present it first, send it second.** I actually broke this rule once on this recent raise, and you know what? I was totally ghosted 👻. And now the cover page of our deck looks... just...like...the...cover...page...of...the...website...of...a...competitive...organization...that...is...a...portfolio...company... of...that...VC. *Shame on you people.*

Enough throat clearing. Here we go:

The Sept 2019 financing round was led by Galaxy Digital Ventures, with participation from Collaborative Fund, CMT Digital, and Avon Ventures, a venture capital fund affiliated with FMR LLC, the parent company of Fidelity Investments. Previous investors True Ventures, Founder Collective, Digital Currency Group, Castle Island, and Boston Seed Capital all participated in this financing round as well.

20 Slides That Raised $7 million:

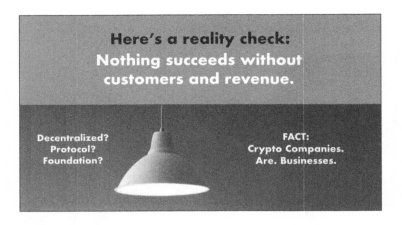

Here's a reality check:
Nothing succeeds without
customers and revenue.

Decentralized?
Protocol?
Foundation?

FACT:
Crypto Companies.
Are. Businesses.

Flipside Crypto
delivers crucial
business intelligence
to help crypto
businesses grow.

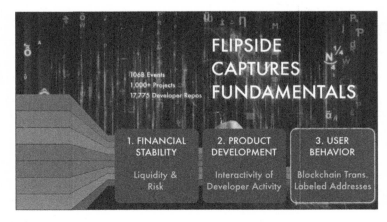

FLIPSIDE
CAPTURES
FUNDAMENTALS

106B Events
1,000+ Projects
17,775 Developer Repos

1. FINANCIAL STABILITY	2. PRODUCT DEVELOPMENT	3. USER BEHAVIOR
Liquidity & Risk	Interactivity of Developer Activity	Blockchain Trans. Labeled Addresses

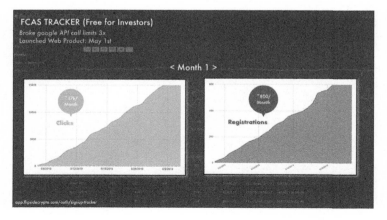

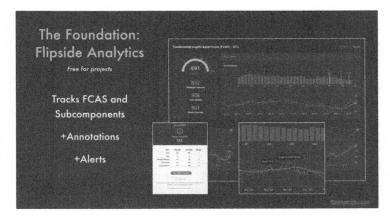

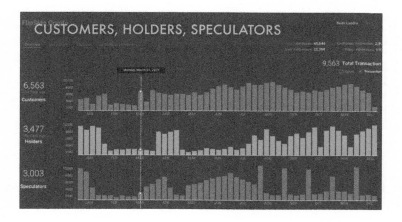

Once ingestion and clustering is complete, Flipside delivers deep insights into activities. We format the data to address three key areas of growth.

Development
Developers and their development patterns.

Users
Customers and how they interact with the project.

Network
The token economy and how it's delivering results

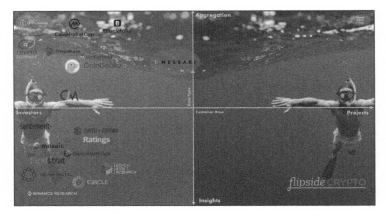

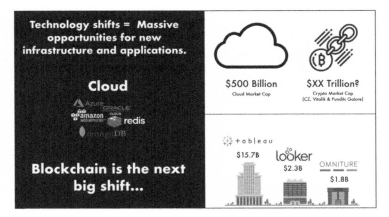

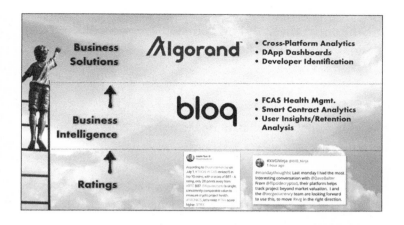

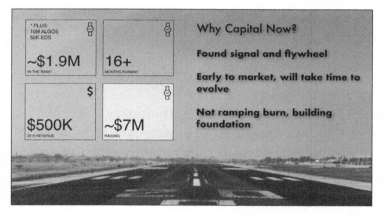

OK, the pitch is over. By now you should be waist-deep in discussions with investors.

THE CLOSE

First things first. Sign that damn term sheet. Nothing happens until that ink is dry.

Second, nothing good happens between signature and close. Your job is to solve every problem, leap over every obstacle, and twist arms to close.

What you'll need:

- **A really good boutique-office lawyer you trust.** For small raises, I try to stay away from the big firms. Call those guys in for massive raises or larger acquisitions.
- **A diligence room with all of your data.** Here's a checklist from Y Combinator: https://blog.ycombinator.com/ ycs-series-a-diligence-checklist/. What? You waited until you signed the term sheet? That's crazy. You should have started during the pitch process.
- **A cap table workbook.** You'll be editing this as investor commitments occur. Everyone will want to know what percentage they will have and who else is in. So be ready to adjust this on the fly. The numbers are rarely final until a few days before close.
- **The flexibility of a yogi master.** Be prepared for anything—changes to investment allocation, a new legal review, a request for a document you don't have, re-pitching, and even lawyer-bickering. Bend to the will of others at times, and at others, make them bend to yours.

POSTSCRIPT: MISTAKES, BROKEN EGGS, AND CELEBRATING

There will be mistakes. Mistakes will happen; it's a willingness to fix them fast that will get the deal done.

Finally, everyone is at the table because they are interested in working together. Remember, in the end, you'll be partners, so crack the eggs, don't break them.

Now, go raise some money. And once you do, keep the celebration light, because that's when the real work begins.

MY WAY—OR THE HIGHWAY

ORIGINALLY PUBLISHED MAY 21, 2019

Late last winter, after just six weeks with the company, one of our employees was floundering.

The issue centered almost entirely on cultural style. The problem?

Cultural leopards rarely change their spots.

This particular employee noted our startup was "weird" and atypical. That we operated oddly, putting the startup at the center of our worlds, and that our constant engagement provided limited time for mental relaxation.

None of that felt odd to us—actually, the rest of the team was so wound around this axle that their fingers would have to be removed with pliers.

That was *our way*. That was *my way*.

The greatest responsibility of any leader is to clarify how talent should behave and deliver, generating unquestionable awareness of how to succeed. No matter how dismal the likelihood this leopard was going to leap into action, the organization was responsible for providing a clear roadmap for potential change.

In cases where there is apparent cultural misalignment from the start, waiting is a kiss of death. It's best to overcommunicate as soon as possible, with an intent to eradicate any cultural misalignment before it festers and creates real pain.

Enter the six-week review.

In this specific case, I provided the G/Y/R,[12] introduced by a two-part approach to success at any startup—and, for certain, any that I happen to be leading.

Here is the approach, exactly as written in the review:

* * *

A TWO-PART APPROACH TO A SUCCESSFUL STARTUP
PART ONE: WAYS OF WORKING

In high school, I was recruited to be a part of the swim team my sophomore year. The swim coach, Pete Foley, had led the team to state championships every year for fifteen years prior to my arrival. My brother was one of the captains, so the general feeling was, genetically, I would be a good swimmer too. I joined the team and worked hard, but basically treated it like it was summer camp.

---

12   G/Y/R stands for Green/Yellow/Red—a written review identifying activities that are great (Greens), activities that show early warning signs of impacting outcomes (Yellows), and activities that are major challenges and need to be fixed immediately (Reds).

In my first race, a fifty-meter breaststroke sprint, I not only finished dead last, but was disqualified for flutter-kicking versus whip-kicking. It was humiliating.

Coach Foley pulled me aside: *"You done donkey-ing around?"*

He noted all of the times I was present yet unwilling to focus on the task at hand. I was the swim-team clown, focused more on generating laughs than results. After he showed me the proper kick, he looked me straight in the eye and made it ultra-clear how the rest of my swimming career would go.

"It's my way or the highway."

By my senior year, I was ranked sixth in the state in the 100-yard breaststroke. I didn't always agree with Coach Foley's way (2,000-yard workouts and a full weight circuit starting at 5:30 a.m. and then, after classes, a return to the pool for 2,000+ more yards), but "his way" was the path to winning the state championships, and that made it all worth it.

Flipside is comprised of individuals whose identity is often driven by their work, which is exhibited by direct and frequent communication, going above and beyond and driving results through true "leadership" in their area of expertise.

That is the Flipside way.

Everyone who works here needs to own that type of cultural DNA or else they'll be constantly at odds with the rest of the organization.

[sic: It's mid-2019 and] Flipside Crypto isn't even a business yet.

It's in the stage where most companies fail. It's in the stage where unwavering dedication is required in order for it to *become* a business.

Having run a number of startups that delivered successful outcomes—and witnessing failure both personally and through the lens of others—I've become incredibly attuned to the behaviors that lead to success.

Organizations fail at this stage often because the vision isn't strong or clear, but way more often because the team isn't owning, driving, crushing, pushing, hitting, nailing, and generally being completely unwilling to accept anything short of success.

You can tell the stage is set for success when every member of the team is pulling well beyond their weight.

They are putting the business first and are lifting up everyone else through their work ethic, communication, and delivery.

Some incredibly important subtext: the behaviors required for today—which generally come down to consistently putting the business first—will evolve over time. Once this amorphous experiment becomes a business, the patterns change and different forms of work/life balance begin to occur.

Net: it won't always be this way, but for the short term, it has to be this way.

It needs to be *my way.*

It's how we win the state championships.

[Postscript: We spent another six months working with this particular leopard and then, unsurprisingly, we parted ways. Looking back, we knew from the start it wasn't going to work. Many will tell you that once you know, you should move fast. Once there's some distance you always ask yourself, *"Why didn't we do that six months earlier?"* That's true. Always. But there are cases where putting in the effort to understand a particular leopard's spots can pay dividends. Then, there are occasions where strong, direct communication about cultural requirements, expectations, and required outcomes will transform someone into a long-term team member. Sometimes—rarely, but sometimes—with the right polish, the spots all align.]

TWO TALES OF TRANSMORAL LEADERSHIP

ORIGINALLY PUBLISHED IN *HACKER NOON*, MAY 30, 2019

So this one entrepreneur commits fraud.

Wait.

I'm getting ahead of myself.

Over the past few years, I've noticed a troubling trend related to moral judgment in the startup world. In an effort to do whatever it takes to succeed—driven by the need to deliver for investors, maintain team respect, or boost personal self-worth—certain entrepreneurs tiptoe over the bright line of ethics and morals with incredible nonchalance.

They justify questionable behavior as part of startup grit.

They aren't morally corrupt all of the time.

Just occasionally. Just the times they need to be.

They are the TransMorals: sometimes they have morals; oftentimes they don't.

I'm not talking about obvious headline-grabbing cases such as Elizabeth from Theranos or Travis from Uber—or even grander, more culturally defining movements such as #metoo—but a more sub-perceptive, cancerous growth that undermines the fundamental underpinnings of entrepreneurship and the startup ecosystem itself.

These behaviors threaten to turn entrepreneurship from a cause of courage—of admirable will and tough risk-taking—into a questionable pursuit driven by those who have more in common with sleight-of-hand card hustlers than authentic magicians.

* * *

So this one entrepreneur commits fraud.

This wasn't so long after he was raised and tenderly cared for by the wolf pack of a well-known accelerator program.

Exactly *why* he did it is obvious: he wanted his startup to succeed, so he cut corners and took risks.

It's no excuse, really.

Frankly, it's stupidity. Ignorance. Ego.

But all that aside, the reality is that he did it because he couldn't come to terms with the fact that his startup might fail.

Exactly *how* he did it is as follows: he stopped paying employee payroll taxes. That's right, he withheld taxes from employee paychecks and failed to deliver them into the hands of the state or federal government. That cash ended up funding the startup's daily cash flow.

So, what about the finance guy—the check and balance—you ask? Well, at the very least, he was a terrible accountant and controller. But more likely, he was culpable and dirty too.

Oh, wait, that's not all. That's not even the fraudulent part.

The company would accept up-front fees from clients who, due to the nature of the offering, had the right to seek a refund—often a year or two later. The fraud: that money was never listed as a liability on the balance sheet. In what amounted to a mini pyramid scheme, millions and millions in raised capital was being utilized to support client refunds versus ongoing operations. Investors may have been in the game, but the leader was bottom-dealing the whole time.

When the lid was blown off this little caper, the CEO hemmed and hawed and seemed confused about why this was a problem. The payroll taxes would eventually be paid, he argued. The undisclosed client liabilities were just poor financial modeling, he shrugged.

The board of directors took immediate action and fired both the CEO and the finance guy. Each had to give their equity back. They never really apologized; they just continued shrugging.

The CEO? He's now a handsomely paid executive at an established major corporation.

The finance guy? He's in law school.

No, really.

* * *

This other entrepreneur, he did it differently.

He ran a cryptocurrency company somewhere around the corner from my office. His company took part in the ICO wave of 2017 and gobbled up a whole pile of investor capital in the form of the cryptocurrency, ETH.

(Of course, they had no actual business to speak of. You know. A b-u-s-i-n-e-s-s: where you sell a product at a higher price than it costs you to make.)

That ETH? It skyrocketed in late 2017, and the firm sold off a huge chunk at three times the value. Timing is, apparently, everything.

Eventually, the Securities and Exchange Commission (SEC) recognized their illicit fundraising efforts by publicly admonishing them for committing securities fraud. In addition, they charged them with registration violations, and required them to pay a hefty fine and refund *every single investor in full.*

So, let's do some math!

Let's say the firm paid all the fines in full. Given the timing of their sell-off, their gain would be in the tens of millions of dollars.

I'm sure you can imagine their bank account. Filled to the brim with garden-soil-brown dirty money.

Shortly after the SEC fine, I was attending a dinner at a local restaurant, and my conversation was repeatedly interrupted by a rowdy table nearby. Whoops and cheers were met with wild fits of laughter. Drinks were being passed around. Glasses clinking.

Waiters were bringing chop after chop of cut meat.

It didn't take long to figure out who the diners were, given most were wearing hoodies emblazoned with the logo of the recently disgraced, SEC-fined firm. The soil was practically falling out of their pockets.

Their CEO deceived investors and broke the law.

Was he removed? Nope. Should the team rebrand? Nope. Should they quietly melt into the woodwork? Nope.

Instead, they should party. They should let everyone know where they work. That they won.

These mongrels considered it a victory.

The problem, though, isn't the entrepreneurs alone: it's the entire technology community's willingness to let grimy, *transmoral* behaviors slide.

In countless cases, investors, shareholders, advisors, team members, and co-founders allow moral injustices to go unchecked, cloaked with the excuse that startups are complex, difficult, and without roadmaps. That risks come with the territory.

Often, in the event that questionable activities do bubble to the surface, no single constituent takes it upon themselves to take action. Transgressing individuals can scoot out the back door for new careers elsewhere or—in the most despicable of cases—remain securely at the helm.

Yet, in the end, no matter how many cleanings or deodorants are applied—no matter how many attempts to wash away sins—the stink of the transmoral leader never dissipates. It just becomes forever embroiled into the fabric of the company.

Maybe they can make a magician's cape with it?

NOTES ON NUTTING UP

ORIGINALLY PUBLISHED IN *HACKER NOON*, SEPTEMBER 8, 2018

We were already forty-three minutes into a thirty-minute call, so now I was late.

I hate being late.

Exasperated and flummoxed, I noted the time and blurted two suggestions:

"First: nut up."

"You're going to be working with an amazing data scientist who can serve as your mentor in a company you seem to really like, in a field you're fascinated by, with a team experienced at creating startups that lead to value creation."

I paused to let that distill.

"Second: I am a sales and M&A guy. I refuse to negotiate against myself, so...you are going to have to tell me exactly what you are asking for."

The air on the other end of the line went cold.

You could literally feel the chill. The relationship we'd been developing through an engaging, transparent, mutually respectful conversation evaporated in milliseconds.

Silence. Then a murmur.

OK, bye then.

"Wait," I offered. *"Where are we?"*

I feel like I'm now on the spot. I'll get back to you.

Then he hung up.

* * *

Let's rewind the tape a bit.

Recruiting is never an easy task, especially if your bar is high in a field that requires ultra-specialized skills.

During our early startup phase, the team at Flipside Crypto decided to add a data scientist to our squad; the right individual would be paired with co-founder Eric Stone—one of the most magnificent data scientists I've ever had the pleasure to work with.

We kicked the process off in earnest. We interviewed dozens of candidates; we kissed a lot of frogs; we spent countless hours coordinating, interviewing, and discussing.

Twice we found individuals we thought would be perfect fits.

In the first case, the candidate showed up fifteen minutes late to our first meeting without even apologizing, but then we were absolutely blown away. She was thoughtful, experienced, and engaged.

Then things got downright weird.

She cancelled a few meetings at the very last minute for family issues in another state; then, well, we found some stuff online that wasn't so becoming. Instead of offering to reschedule, we politely offered her a way to "press pause" due to the family stuff—and she agreed.

Months of work, and still no resource. We were beyond disappointed.

Then we met another candidate who was quirky and brilliant. We gave him the exercise we provide to candidates and...damn, he flubbed it. Argh.

We were honest. We provided a treasure trove of feedback, and—whaddya know—he responded incredibly well. He showed true ability to sponge our information and expressed how excited he was to take his skills to a new level.

Then, suddenly, he withdrew his candidacy. He offered something about wanting more flexibility in a remote role—but was super critical of a typo on our website (for real).

We were crushed. Another month of work down the drain.

"Hire slow, fire fast" is what they say.

What they don't say is the only way to do that is to beat off desperation with a big friggin' stick.

Then we met our most recent candidate.

So...shall we call him *Mr. Nut Up?*

He was new to Boston, and after some time in the military, had spent a few years at a global corporation comprised of hundreds of thousands of employees. After passing all of our phone screens, he completely crushed the exercise.

He said it took him twenty to forty hours, an oddly broad range (especially for a data scientist), but this didn't seem to be a showstopper. He came in for a few hours of interviews; the chemistry was obvious. The fit seemed...perfect.

But here was the rub: he had an offer in hand from another company and had to determine if he was going to take that in a few days.

Together, we agreed to shortcut the process: he came in for another whiteboard session, and we concurrently arranged immediate reference checks. It felt rushed, frenetic. We couldn't possibly get to know each other in such a short time, but...the clock was ticking.

Eventually, we determined he was worthy of pursuit. We outlined a cash and option package (larger than his other offer) and enthusiastically told him if he wanted the job, it was his to have.

The next day, an email.

[Subject:] Accepting the Flipside Crypto Offer.

After much deliberation, I have decided to choose Flipside Crypto. Know that the decision was not easy. However, I recognize a rare opportunity when I see one. But that alone was not enough to sway me. I was impressed by the outstanding team and the character of its members. I consider it an honor to be part of Flipside Crypto and will do my best going forward.

Thrilled, we fired off an official offer. He responded enthusiastically but asked if I would mind helping him understand how equity and options worked in startups. Easy peasy.

The next morning, we hopped on the phone. He started by asking about the vesting structure, but then moved quickly to an outline of the option package's potential value based solely on our last exit (Smarterer @ $75M pre-IPO). All fair and valid things to probe—and the conversation was fluid and upbeat.

But the questions continued.

Would there be additional grants? (Absolutely, when we hit milestones.)

Was his amount of shares in line with others? (Yes, actually maybe a bit on the higher side.)

Would there be acceleration if we were acquired? (Yes, that often happens.)

After twenty minutes, the questions became less clear, less direct, and less obvious.

We began going in circles. Ten more minutes.

He stammered and paused. I kept asking him what he actually wanted. I hinted that maybe it was a larger option grant? He kept reiterating the same questions. He hemmed and hawed. He said he was trying to compare his option package to a 401(k) he might receive at a larger company.

More circles. More pauses.

Then, I broke. I couldn't handle the indecisiveness. The lack of clarity. I couldn't handle what felt like a fishing expedition in pea-soup-like fog.

My brain flashed "nut up," a phrase I first heard uttered by Woody Harrelson in *Zombieland*.

Before thinking, I said it out loud. I followed up with some logic around how we ensure employees are compensated with fairness and that, at some point, he is going to have to either trust us or not.

An hour later, an email:

> *You have a great company and will no doubt find the talent you need to succeed. This truly was a difficult decision for me, but at the end of the day, I don't feel like this is the place for me. I apologize for my lack of certainty and wish you the best in your search.*

I've hired hundreds of employees over the years and it never gets easy. You can practice, you can study, you can learn. But you will always be a student.

Having reflected on this recent situation, I'm reminded of a number of important lessons for any hiring process:

- **Damn it, never (ever) cut corners.** There are always time constraints and reasons to rush. Rushing often leads to mis-hires or a poorly constructed relationship.
- **Reference checks are not box checks.** One reference noted the candidate "could be stubborn, especially when it came to communicating with the business side of organizations." A red flag. In this case, overlooked and ignored because we were rushing.
- **Never underestimate people's ability to fool themselves.** In a postmortem (after declining the offer), the candidate later admitted he "started second-guessing himself the minute he sent the email accepting the offer."
- **Hire communicators.** If someone isn't able to frame their needs, you'll always be a step away from the truth.
- **A deal isn't done until it's done.** I've had new hires fail to show up for the first day of work. No matter how sure you are, there are always surprises.

Finally, don't ever tell a candidate to "nut up." That should be obvious.

Turns out class is still in session.

SHORTER FLIGHTS AT LOWER HEIGHTS: THE RIGHT WAY TO ANGEL INVEST

ORIGINALLY PUBLISHED IN DHARMESH SHAH'S *ONSTARTUPS*, JULY 12, 2012

Careful now, because everywhere you step these days, you might tread on an angel investor.

Aside from those who have always invested small amounts of cash in startups, more and more venture capitalists are making personal side deals, active entrepreneurs are investing in other entrepreneurs, pre-pre-seed funds are cropping up, and Angel-List has become deal flow for the everyman.

But here's a reality: most angel investors will fail. Hard. They'll fail to even return the capital they invested, let alone make money. And it's not because they don't pick good companies or back great entrepreneurs—it's because they're completely mistaken about an angel investor's role in the investing cycle.

There are a clear set of boundaries that guide the startup

investing ecosystem: angel investors (angels) get things started, venture capitalists (VCs) create mature, sustainable businesses, and investment bankers sell companies or take them public.

The problem: many angels confuse themselves with VCs. They:

- Seek 10× home-run acquisitions
- Agree to follow-on investments (pro-rata or more), often through multiple rounds
- Invest in game-changing ideas that are incredibly risky
- Hold out for companies to get acquired or go public for their return

But the punchline is obvious. Angels aren't venture capitalists. They don't have the deal flow. They don't have the limited partners to answer to. They aren't paid a management fee to take bets. And there are things VCs are great at that angels should avoid at all costs, like waiting eons for markets to evolve, sitting on boards, or making decisions on whether to replace founders and CEOs who aren't thriving.

An angel's role is to enable entrepreneurs to begin, to capitalize them when the only people willing to give them money are friends and family. They should make bets where the VCs won't play—like on ideas on napkins from first-time founders, or in industries that may not have obvious scale.

If angels want to win, they'll take a simpler route: they'll *fly shorter flights at lower heights.*

Shorter flights: seeking early exits for their investment capital, usually at a future venture investment round. Lower heights: not aiming for billion-dollar outcomes or finding the next five Facebooks, Ubers, or Pelotons.

An angel investor should:

- Aim for a two- to four-times return (vs. 10x)
- Get out of deals in one to three years, selling their shares to VCs at the series A or B venture rounds (and not feel bad about it)
- Understand that they're playing with their own money versus risking someone else's via a fund they've raised
- Remember that angel investing isn't about charity work; if someone wishes to spend money helping others, they should find a good cause and donate to that instead

Take this route, and angels will actually help more entrepreneurs achieve their dreams—all while lowering the investment risk and generating better returns. The benefits compound upon each other:

- **Risk reduction.** Money loss is rarely because the company goes out of business in the first few years. Rather, it's because the company matures and becomes more difficult to sustain through ups and downs. Getting out early will allow an angel to get more out, more often.
- **Maximize funding companies.** The majority of angels have the ability to invest in just a handful of deals, let's say ten at a maximum. If an angel exits from one or two in the short term, that two to four times return will allow them to back more entrepreneurs and launch more companies, more often.
- **Avoid dilution to nothing.** One of the major issues in

angel investing is that a successful company often goes through many rounds of funding at higher and higher valuations. Often at that stage, VCs don't provide early angels the ability to invest, and even more often angels can't invest due to the financial commitment (they will get asked to invest at down rounds, which doesn't really work, given limited capital from angels). The result: an angel is left diluted to a meaningless percentage, so the outcome becomes negligible.

· **Stay in the know.** In the successful company scenario, the outcome is even bleaker. The major investors no longer provide early investors with information rights (the right to receive financial or strategic facts about the company). The entrepreneur moves on to focus on their board, their venture investors, and their company. That leaves most angels with a variety of companies that they're entirely clueless about.

· **Provide venture capitalists with more ownership.** When a company begins to succeed, institutional investors want as much ownership as they can get. Without lowering valuation, this conflicts with founders, who also wish to maintain their ownership percentage. The solution: angels should sell shares to the VCs as part of future rounds. The VCs receive more ownership, angels make money, and entrepreneurs limit dilution. Win-win-win.

· **Relieve VCs and acquirers from having to deal with angels.** VCs want clean, simple capitalization tables (fewer people involved = fewer headaches) and acquirers don't want to have to deal with shareholder lawsuits or other risks of having a whole bunch of (relatively) unsophisticated investors involved. The fewer angels involved later, the better.

Again, this is really just about angels agreeing to be what they really are: earlier-stage investors who are extending their own capital to develop new companies. Angel investing is special, but it shouldn't be confused with running a venture fund or delivering venture-scale returns for limited partners.

Everyone needs to play along: funded entrepreneurs need to be supportive of angels who seek to sell their ownership during a later A or B round; venture capitalists need to be willing to purchase shares from angels during these rounds; and angels need to stick to their role.

To the angel investors: aim shorter and lower. You'll receive better returns and support more companies.

Which is the point after all, isn't it?

TO BE A GREAT LEADER, DON'T BE A GENIUS; BE A SPONGE AND A STONE

ORIGINALLY PUBLISHED IN *FORBES*, SEPTEMBER 15, 2011

There's a misconception that many successful business leaders achieve greatness because of their intellect. One might glance at leaders like Sheryl Sandberg, Reed Hastings, and Warren Buffett, and judge those rumors to be true. Yep, they're insanely smart—geniuses even—and in all likelihood, yep, they're more successful than you. A correlation that would point to the level of smarts to define success.

Given this, maybe you should just hang up your leadership spurs right now and find some other walk of life.

No so fast. Fret not; this relationship isn't the norm.

In fact, most highly successful leaders are far from the smartest people in the room. Rather, their success has very little to do with the horsepower of their smarts. The secret to their success is something they had to learn, hone, and refine over time. It's a set of behaviors that enables them to maximize the results of whatever level of intellect they have.

That secret that sets them apart? It's *the sponge and the stone.*

You'll come across sponges and stones in every organization, at every level of seniority.

They'll distinguish themselves by their capacity, by the sheer volume of work they can accomplish, and by their spirit: their willingness to accept any task and deliver at 110 percent. And by the fact that just about any team, just about anywhere would want to have them in just about any role.

One can be a sponge *or* a stone, but it's the sponge and the stone—the two together—that can transform the everyday citizen into a force of nature.

The order of operations matters. Sponging always comes first.

Sponges are individuals who are tirelessly driven to seek and absorb new information. They are highly curious—possibly bordering on obsessive—about gathering data and learning.

Sponges exhibit the following behaviors. They:

- **Learn from mentors, advisors, and peers.** Sponges surround themselves with people who offer insights and external points of view. They build and tap strong advisor networks. Sponges will seek out managers that inspire them—that they can learn from. Sponges ask questions and soak up the answers.
- **Study heroes.** A sponge will watch heroes and adapt their

skills based on what they observe. An early hero of mine was the Russian novelist Vladimir Nabokov. While I appreciated his novels, I found myself more obsessed with his writing process: Nabokov produced novels utilizing index cards, which he would arrange and rearrange until the flow of the words fit together with perfection. I sponged that habit and now write out speeches on index cards to organize and reshuffle to best suit the narrative. Nabokov compared the way he wrote to building a bird's nest, and claimed that his notes made up a "kaleidoscopic arrangement of broken impressions." This deeply informed my view that developing a company is the establishment of a set of elements that, together, eventually form the safe foundation for growth—much like a bird's nest.

- **Read voraciously.** Sponges tend to consume the written word, heavily. Some focus on Twitter blasts or LinkedIn updates. Others prefer long form and are voracious consumers. Katie Burke, chief people officer at HubSpot, read one hundred books in 2019. Some devour business books, others enjoy fantasy or fiction, and a few may obsess over every detail in an instruction manual from IKEA. It doesn't matter the form or length of the content; a sponge will thirst for as much information as possible.

The act of sponging delivers an obvious result: continuous education, lifelong learning, and ultimately, individual growth and evolution. It's what the sponge does with this learning that completes the equation. Completion relies on becoming the stone.

There are two main characteristics of stone behavior:

- **Commitment to hard work.** Stones are relentlessly committed to the effort required to succeed. They probably work harder than you. They will consistently ignore shortcuts, and they aren't bound by the time of day or day of the week. They often can't outsmart, but they can outwork. This may resonate as the skill for those who have the gift of youth on their side; those who have a lack of responsibilities, time, and unbound energy. Someone who is fine to eat ramen three nights a week and is happy to sleep on a blow-up mattress. But consider Sidney Frank, who at the ripe age of seventy-seven, founded Grey Goose Vodka. He spent countless hours acting as the stone—working tirelessly to craft one of the world's most recognized brands—and he sold it five years later for $2 billion. Sidney was already wealthy from previous ventures, and while he may have been scrappy, he was also probably sleeping on 600-thread-count Egyptian cotton sheets while building Grey Goose. Stones come in all shape and sizes.

- **Strength of conviction.** A stone's willingness to execute is only matched by their unwavering belief in their pursuit and the readiness to drive through walls regardless of the challenges, hurdles, naysayers, and failures they encounter. When we launched BzzAgent, we were thrown out of at least a dozen advertising and marketing agencies in Boston. We were berated for the silliness of our idea, for not understanding how marketing worked, and for not knowing what brands needed to succeed. (I will never forget being escorted out of advertising firm Hill Holliday just fifteen minutes into our pitch.) Yet we persisted. Above all else, we believed. We were unabashed in our conviction that what we were building would work. Stones don't need convincing.

For those who exhibit both sponge and stone behavior, you're likely to witness the following:

- **Fearlessness—even shamelessness.** Stones don't just work 24/7; they work every angle. Consider Rajat Suri, the founder of Presto, which makes tabletop ordering systems for restaurants. He once recommended that I check out a Palo Alto sushi joint because of a long-held rumor that Steve Jobs occasionally dined at the Omakase counter. As luck would have it, Jobs walked in halfway through the meal. Respecting his private space, I snapped a pic of him from afar, paid my bill, and left, eventually emailing Raj to let him know the rumors were true. What did Raj—tireless opportunist and stone—do? He dashed to the restaurant, secured a seat next to Jobs, and started toying around with an early version of his Presto device as the Apple chief looked over his shoulder and commented on the interface.
- **Belief that the impossible is possible.** When my partners and I founded BzzAgent, my fourth startup, we were turned down by nearly 200 different investors. My family was so concerned about the unlikelihood of success that they staged an intervention, where they sat me down and tried to talk me out of pursuing the business. Three years later we were generating $3 million in revenue, were profitable, and had raised our first round of outside capital. With lessons from sponging everything I could about word-of-mouth marketing, and a rock-solid tenacity to make things happen, we literally willed the business into existence.
- **Multiple plates spinning.** Sponges and stones, by their nature, have incredible curiosity and, often, ideas and energy to burn. For example, Elon Musk runs Tesla but also leads SpaceX. And Jack Dorsey leads Twitter, but also is running Square, his digital payments platform. One of the greatest errors an investor, advisor, or mentor can make is to try to force a multitasking stone to rein things in. Exploring additional projects allows the sponge to con-

stantly learn, and the stone in them will seek out additional initiatives: multitasking is often a signal of sponge-and-stone DNA.

In all likelihood, you're probably not the next Jeff Bezos or Indra Nooyi. And, maybe you're not the next Bill Gates or Kenneth Chenault.

Don't despair.

Listen. Become the Sponge.

Dig deep. Become the Stone.

Success is just a matter of time.

6 MOMENTS TO MARRIAGE

ORIGINALLY PUBLISHED IN *P.S. I LOVE YOU*, JUNE 6, 2017

On June 5, 2017, I surprise-married Sarah Hodges.

OK, it wasn't a surprise to us. And, well, it probably wasn't a surprise to most who know us.

So, maybe this is better:

On June 5, 2017, I married Sarah Hodges.

The path to marriage is a symphony of moments and milestones. The significance of some are immediate and obvious, but the majority are everyday moments that achieve meaning only through the passing of time and reflection.

Here are six that matter.

* * *

I. THE DAVE BALTER TECH PROM

Back in September 2011, Sarah Hodges infamously jump-started a Tech Prom, by marketing one—unbeknownst to me—with my name on it.

Mike Troiano, Sarah Hodges, Dave Balter, Jen Lum, Cort Johnson: your Tech Prom committee

Eventually, a committee of five (Mike Troiano, Jennifer Lum, Cort Johnson, Sarah, and I) joined forces to raise $85,000 from the likes of Wayfair, Softlayer, GSN, and Boston Seed Capital. We threw an open bar, dress-up-and-get-down rager just thirty days later.

Sarah had a boyfriend at the time, and I was married. There wasn't anything romantic about the countless hours of planning and organizing, but there was little doubt that our energy was magnetic.

Sarah actually spent most of the evening miffed at me for over-inviting guests and possibly getting us shut down. I was mainly oblivious (hell, this was a party with my name on it!), which only stirred the pot.

At about 1 a.m., the evening was over, and by all accounts it was an incredible success. I went home to bed. I was tucked into a deep sleep when the phone buzzed.

It's Sarah. It's 3 a.m.

"Have you seen my computer? I can't find it!" She was frantic. Exasperated.

The first person she thought to call was me.

In the immortal words of Robert Hunter (to a melody set by Jerry Garcia) from *Terrapin Station*:

> *I can't figure out if it's the end or beginning...*

✳ ✳ ✳

2. THE SEXY BEAST OF SPAIN

Sarah and I—and a number of friends and my daughter Stella—spent three weeks in Spain in the summer of 2013.

This wasn't just any Spain. It was Comares, an off-the-grid, out-of-a-magazine, bleached-white village sitting on the top of a mountain.

Why there? Because I'd remarked—in passing—that *Sexy Beast* was one of my favorite movies and that the location in the heat-drenched hills of southern Spain seemed fascinating. Like a place I'd just want to be.

So Sarah—make-it-happen Sarah—figured out the general area of Spain, researched dozens of possible houses, outlined travel logistics, and set about planning the trip of a lifetime.

Sarah and Leila near Comares, Spain

How could you not love someone willing to fulfill even the most random dreams?

* * *

3. A CASE OF SPANISH BEDBUGS

Sarah believed she had carried a trove of bedbugs back from our Spain trip.

One morning at 7 a.m., she called me from the lobby of a hotel where she remarked she'd been working since 4 a.m.

The story goes like this:

She had woken in the middle of the night, apparently feeling bugs all over her. She turned the lights on and could swear she saw bugs moving. Maybe. Or...maybe...she couldn't really be sure. But she did what anyone else who thought they might have bedbugs in the middle of the night would do. She bagged up her sheets and *all* of her clothes, and jettisoned them into some dumpsters in the Back Bay.

No, really, *all* of her clothes.

In a pre-dawn rainstorm, she found a twenty-four-hour CVS and bought stretch pants and an oversized Hanes T-shirt—and started her wardrobe over.

Bedbugs or not, if there's one thing about Sarah: when she commits, she commits.

God, it's enviable.

✳ ✳ ✳

4. INDIA

We went to India on a business trip and ate the food.

Now Sarah believes she has a permanent tapeworm.

Not quite the threesome I'd been hoping for.

* * *

5. WE ♥ TOUR

One year, Phish was booked to play their New Year's run at Madison Square Garden. Having never really listened to Phish—but realizing I'm fanatical, having seen north of 400 shows since 1990—Sarah agrees to go on the thirtieth to check it out, with plans to have a quiet evening alone at her hotel on the thirty-first.

"I'll see just one night," she said. *"Besides, New Year's is for amateurs."*

Three songs in and she's begging me, relentlessly, over and over, *"How do we get a ticket for me for tomorrow night?"*

The next summer, we went on tour—an activity usually reserved for those with few responsibilities or reckless youth—catching sixteen shows.

Only Sarah would go all in, all the way.

Sarah Hodges, on tour

In Trey Anastasio's (and his lyrical wingman, Tom Marshall's) words, from the song *Waste*:

a dream it's true

but I'd see it through

if I could be

wasting my time with you

* * *

6. IT'S ALWAYS A DANCE PARTY

Recently, we were in Florida with our kids, enjoying some sun. Shortly after dinner, we turned on the music and, lo and behold, the evening devolved into an all-out dance party. Sarah, Stella, and Annie—at ages eleven and eight, respectively—traded moves.

Running man!

Shim Sham!

Do the lawnmower.

Take it off the shelf.

A dance party with your entire family—what is this, Pleasantville?

Flash back to a few weeks before. Same location, but this time with adults in tow—the music comes on even earlier. And so does the dancing.

The next morning, one of our guests remarked, *"I honestly thought dance parties like that only happened in the movies."*

In the summer of 2015, we rented a house in Truro, Massachusetts. This time, the dancing was hard to contain.

It moved from the kitchen to the living room. It meandered its way to the porch outside. In the frenzy, Sarah found a bench behind a floor-to-ceiling window that looked out over the living room.

Fully in the moment, Sarah did what only Sarah would do—she got up and danced. Solo. For a good ten minutes, for everyone else. She destroyed.

With Sarah, you're always free to dance.

* * *

Meow.

End of this story, but clearly the beginning of many stories to come.

Please meet my wife: Sarah Hodges.

Sarah Hodges and Dave Balter

POSTSCRIPT: TWO
STAND-INS

SEEKING: (CONTENT) BUSINESS DEVELOPMENT DIRECTOR, CONTENT

ORIGINALLY PUBLISHED JUNE 9, 2015

The Pluralsight transactions team is seeking that special someone for that special something from that special place.

- Loves to cut the rug, cut the crap and—most of all—cut the deal.
- Sniffs out so much big prey that Afrin is a sponsor.
- *Is* content. Like happy. And *knows* content, like online learning. One might say they are content with the content, or the content makes them content. You pick.
- Technically astute; occasionally irons shirts; never needs to solder chips.
- Knows that edtech never brought sexy back.
- Always says always. Never says never. One documented instance of maybe.
- Peter picked a pepper of a people person.
- At least 7+ years of experience. Hopefully not the only years, because we do not hire anyone under eight.

- Often humorous, rarely offended (except by Bobcat Goldthwait).

Join our team because you love what you do. And because we pay you money, provide unlimited vacation, and make your life easy with 100 percent healthcare coverage.

We also offer unlimited snacks. Personally, I like beef jerky.

[This role was filled by the energetic, effective, and amazingly named Cooper Moo.]

WANTED: NOT-AN-ASS ASSOCIATE

ORIGINALLY PUBLISHED NOVEMBER 18, 2013

dunnhumby is seeking a venture associate who likes to be loved, and loves to be liked.

- Instinctually adept, financially sound, analytically neo-phytical (not to be confused with necrophylical).
- Hunts on the savannah of startups, with email, Twitter, and LinkedIn as weapons.
- Vitamix 5000s lunch meat to slurp calories while taking phone calls.
- Drives shockingly fast, but always uses turn signals.
- Likes to gamble; loves to raise. Can't bluff for shit.
- Lists, catalogs, inventories, registers, records, itemizes. And again.
- Is. Not. Annoying.
- Does. Not. Have. Halitosis.
- Why are you reading this right now and not out meeting people?

[This position was filled by Kyle Fugere. Who almost didn't get the job until he offhandedly walked us through a story about getting deathly sick in rural Africa. The village he was staying in (he was on a humanitarian mission) had little by way of medical supplies, so he was carried for miles to a church where he was dumped on the steps. He sweltered in the heat for hours before the church opened and they took him in to provide medical care. He reflected that story with magical a gleam in his eye. With so much thankfulness for the experience—and so much humility—that he was hired on the spot.]

ABOUT THE AUTHOR

DAVE BALTER is CEO of Flipside Crypto, which provides business intelligence to crypto organizations. Previously, Dave was co-founder and CEO of Smarterer, a skills assessment company acquired by Pluralsight (NASDAQ: PS) in 2014. Post-acquisition, Dave was head of transactions at Pluralsight, while also serving as a board observer. In 2001, Dave founded and was CEO of BzzAgent, a social media marketing company, which was acquired by dunnhumby, a division of Tesco, in 2011. From 2011 to 2014, Dave sat on the Global Executive Team at dunnhumby, where he led all M&A activity and founded and led their investment arm, dunnhumby Ventures. Dave is Venture Partner Emeritus at Boston Seed Capital; personally, he is an investor or advisor to more than fifty technology organizations.

Made in the USA
Coppell, TX
17 August 2020

33463412R00142